MUSE

THE 2ND LAW

Music Arranged by Olly Weeks

Edited by Lucy Holliday

Book Design by Chloë Alexander

Neuro images supplied courtesy of the Human Connectome Project,
Laboratory of Neuro Imaging, UCLA

Band Photography by Gavin Bond

ISBN 1-978-4803-3774-9

HAL•LEONARD® CORPORATION

7777 W. BLUEMOUND RD. P.O. BOX 13819 MILWAUKEE, WI 53213

Visit Hal Leonard Online at

www.halleonard.com

muse.mu

Contents

SUPREMACY

Words and Music by Matthew Bellamy

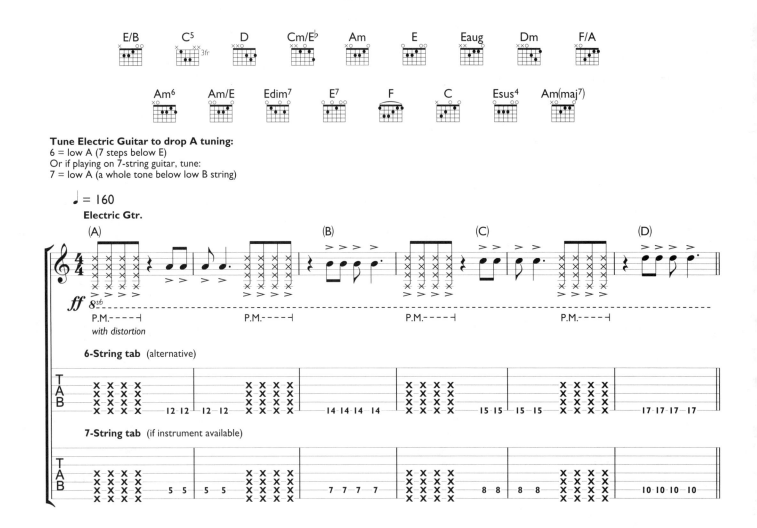

Tune Electric Guitar to drop A tuning:
6 = low A (7 steps below E)
Or if playing on 7-string guitar, tune:
7 = low A (a whole tone below low B string)

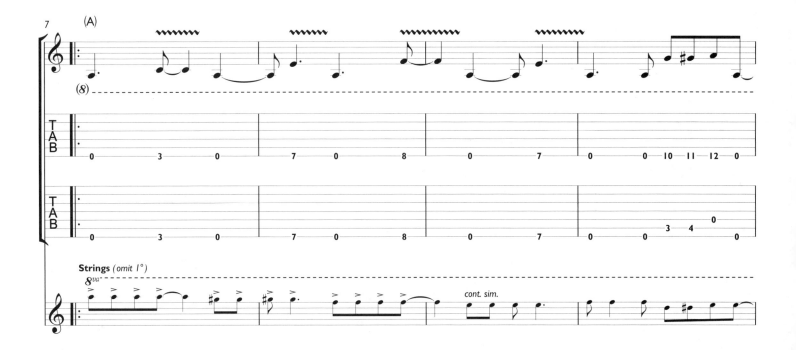

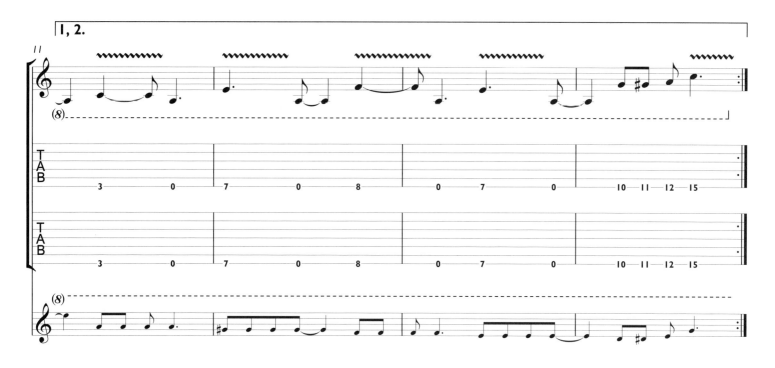

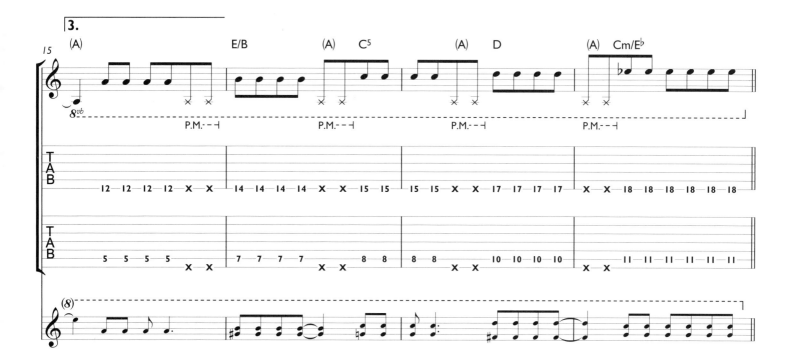

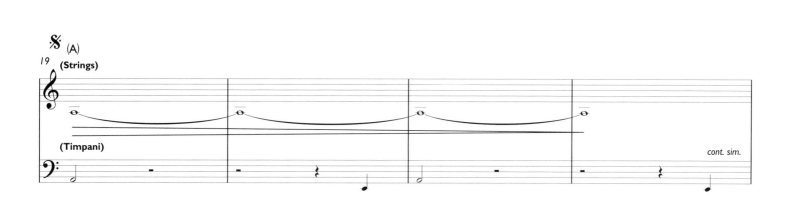

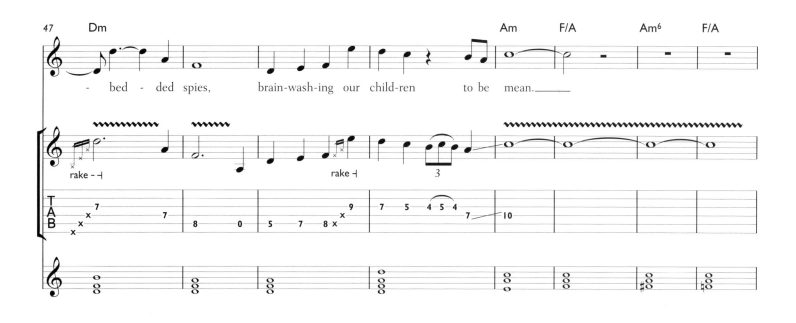

- bed - ded spies, brain-wash-ing our child-ren to be mean.____

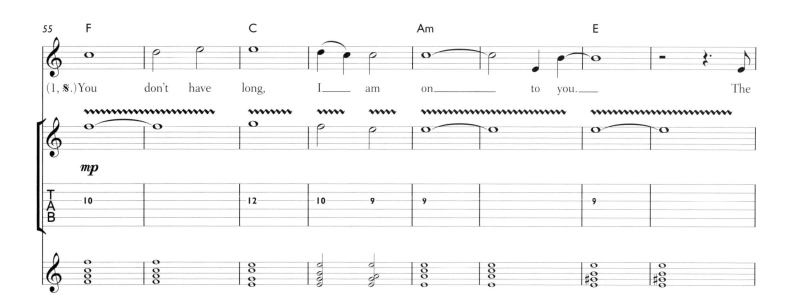

(1, %.)You don't have long, I____ am on_____ to you.____ The

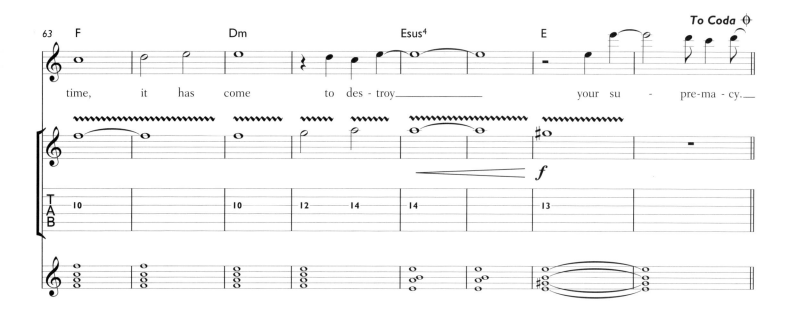

time, it has come to des - troy_____ your su - pre-ma - cy.____

Yeah,   yeah,__ yeah,____ yeah, yeah,   yeah,__ yeah,____ yeah,   yeah,_ yeah, yeah,_ yeah, yeah..

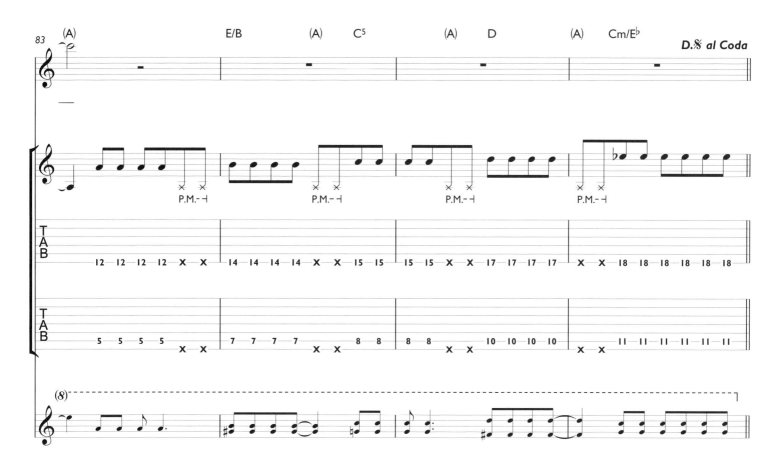

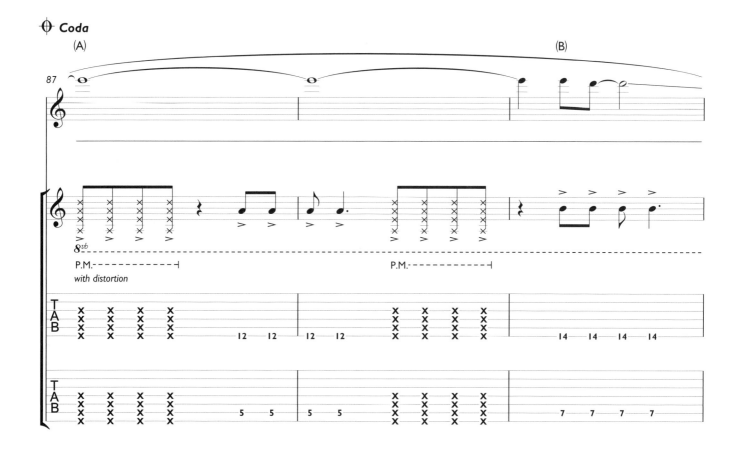

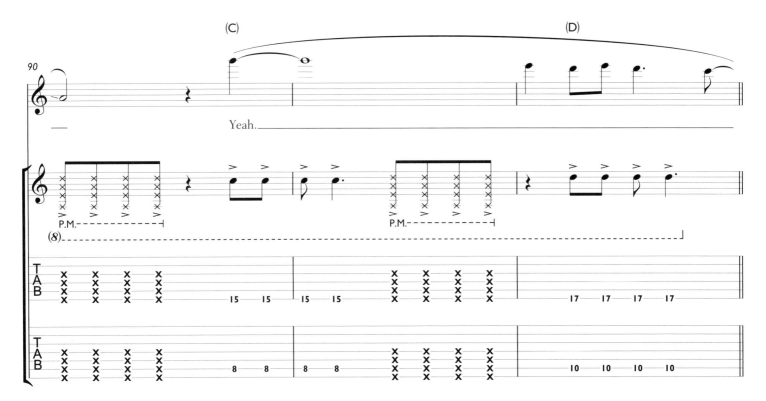

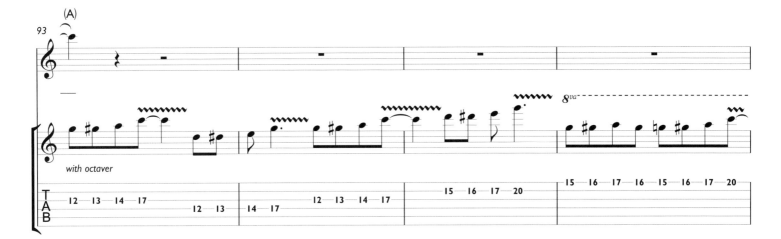

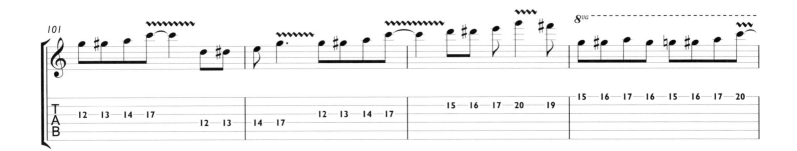

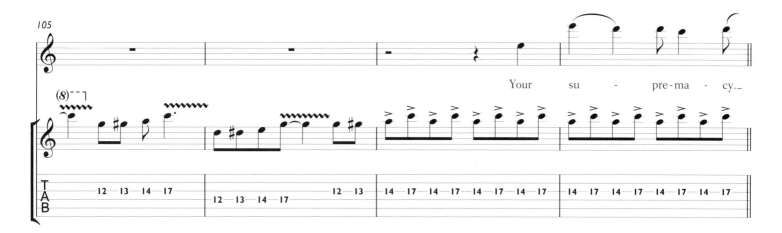

Your su - pre-ma - cy.__

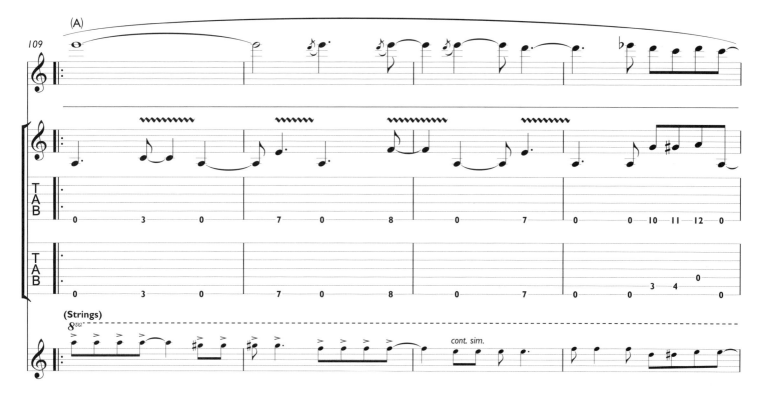

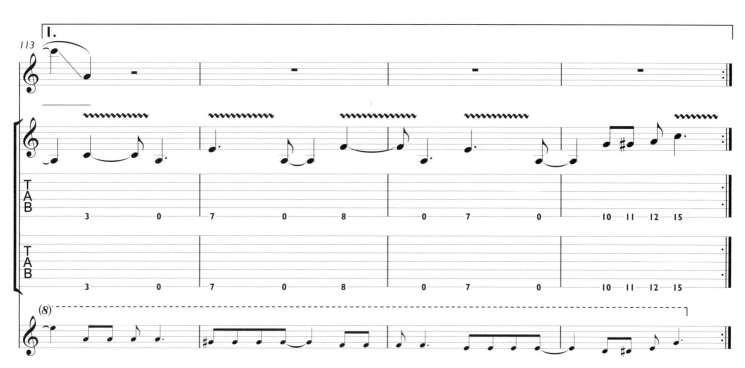

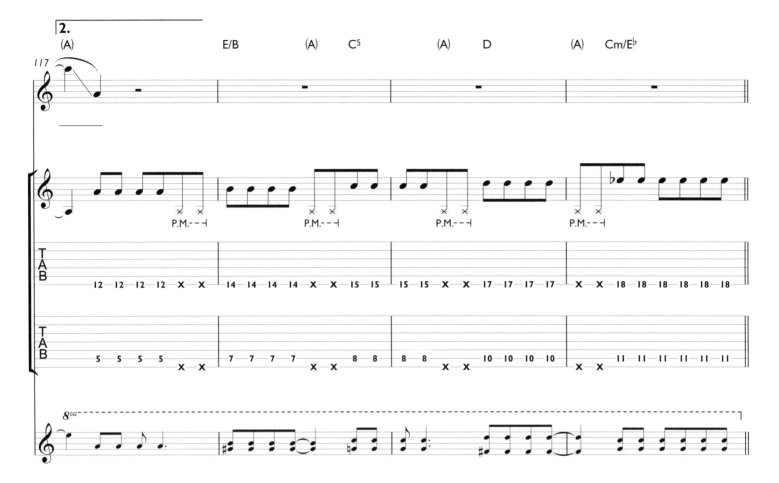

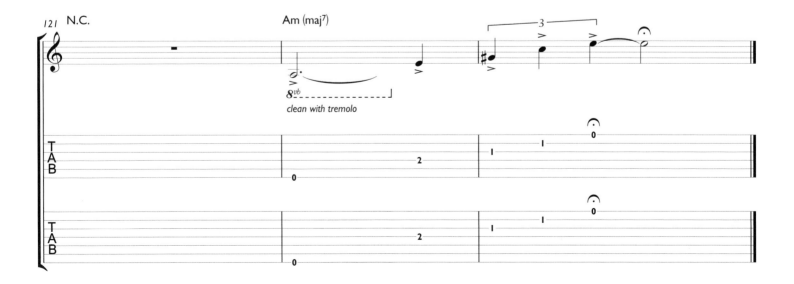

MADNESS

Words and Music by Matthew Bellamy

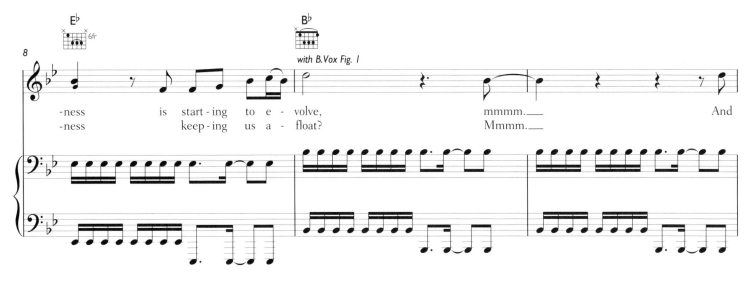

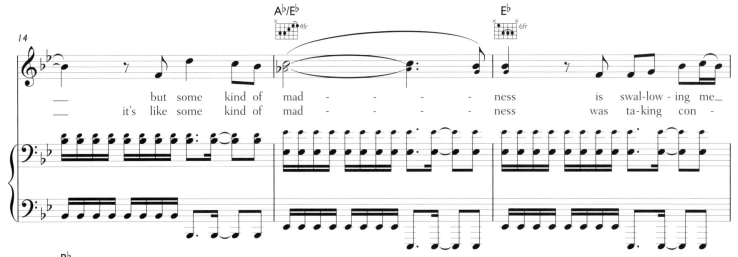

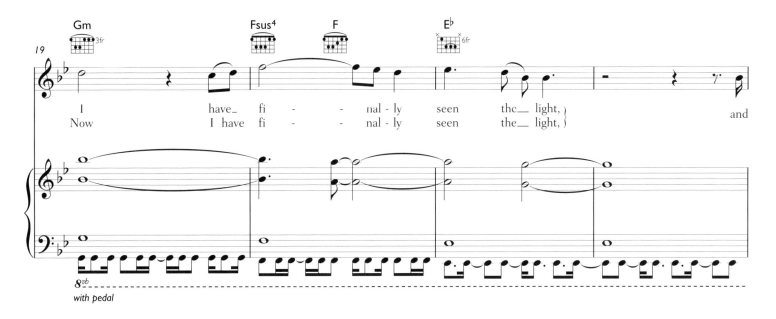

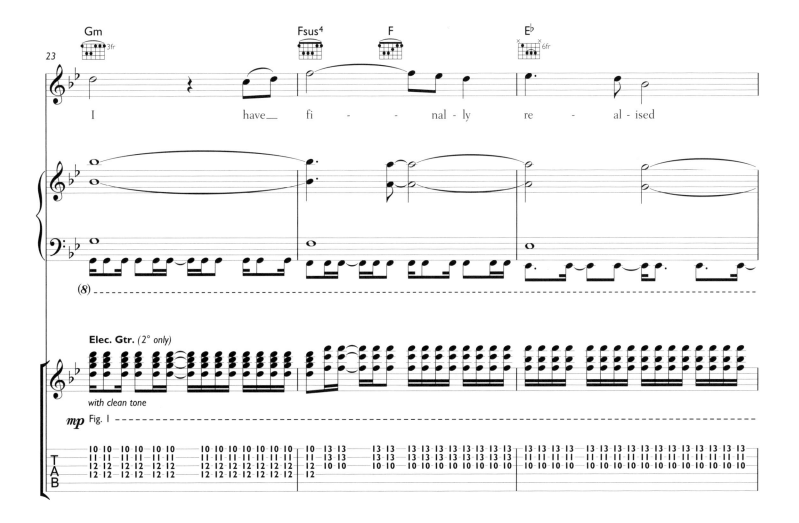

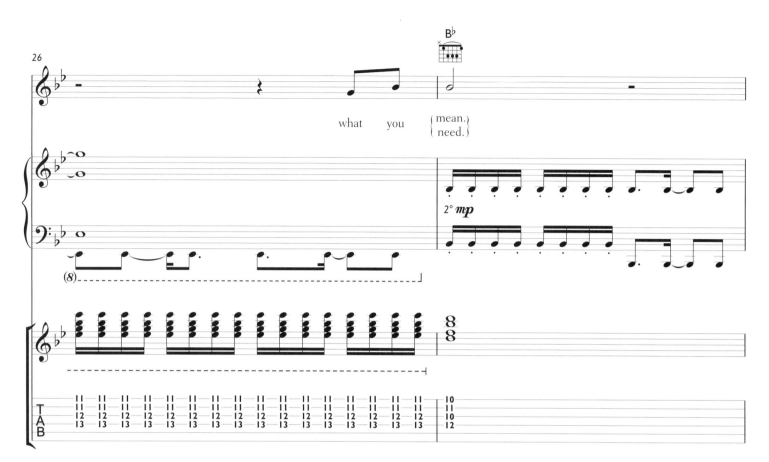

what you {mean.}
{need.}

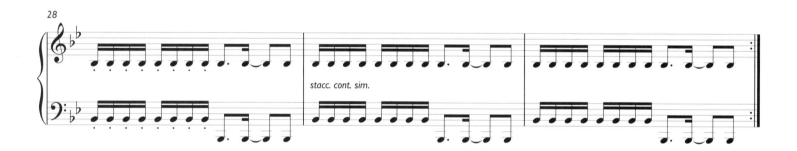

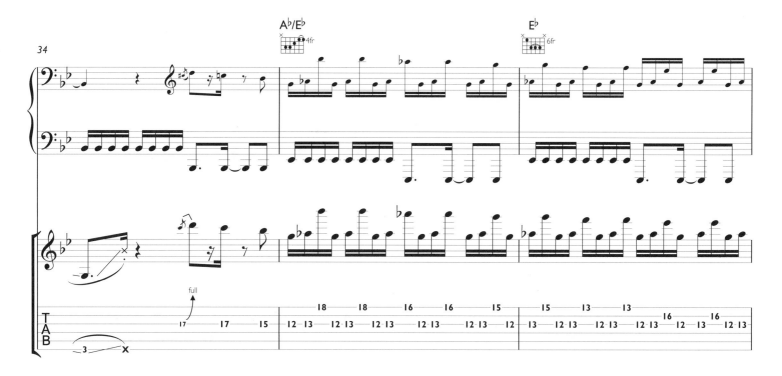

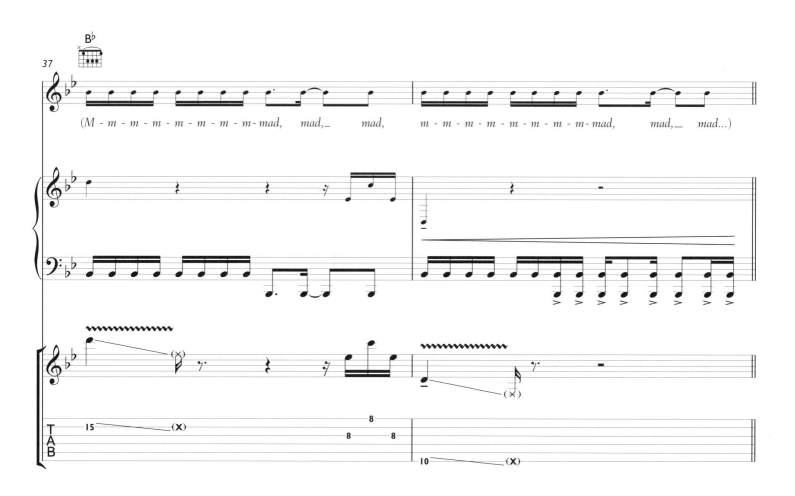

(M - m - m - m - m - m - m - m - mad,   mad,__   mad,   m - m - m - m - m - m - m - m - mad,   mad,__   mad...)

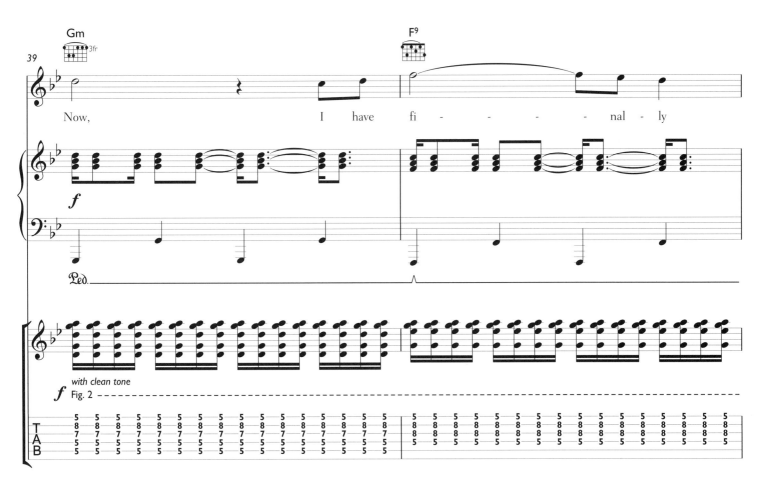

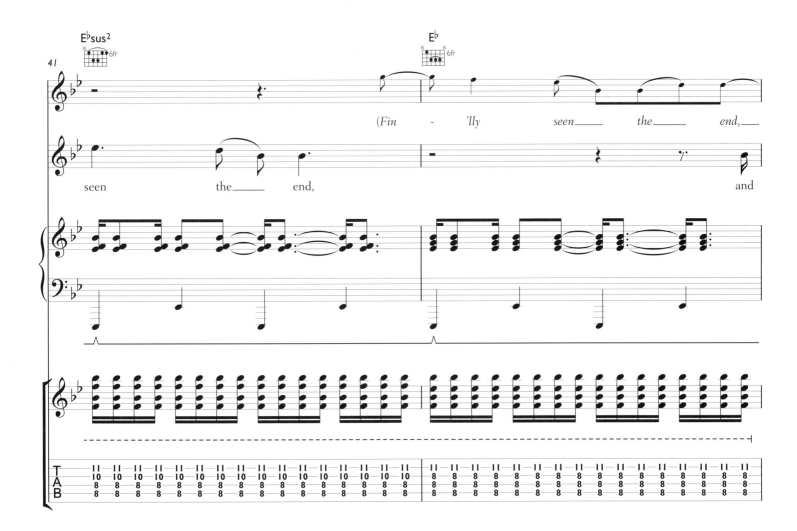

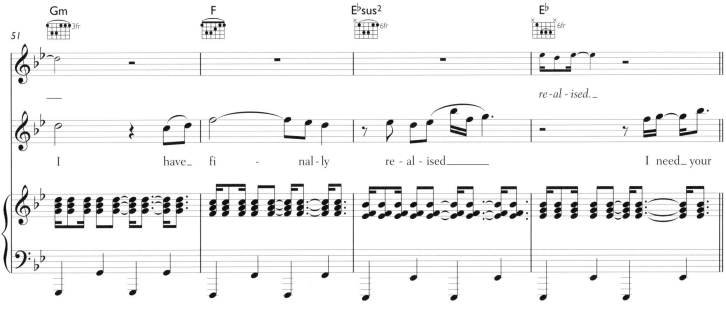

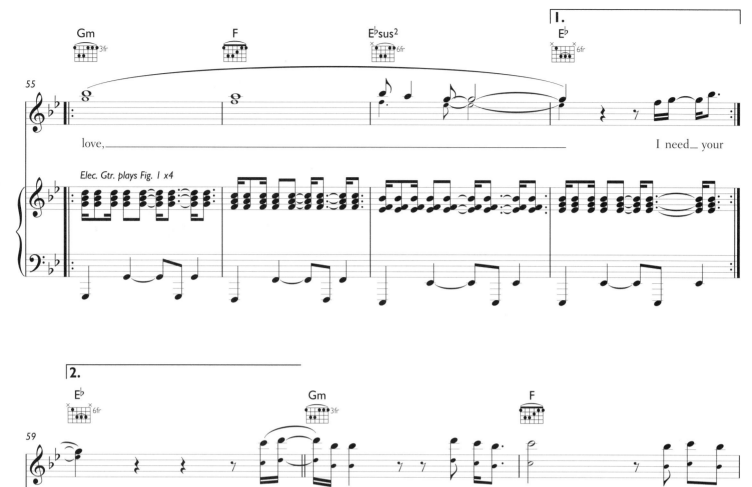

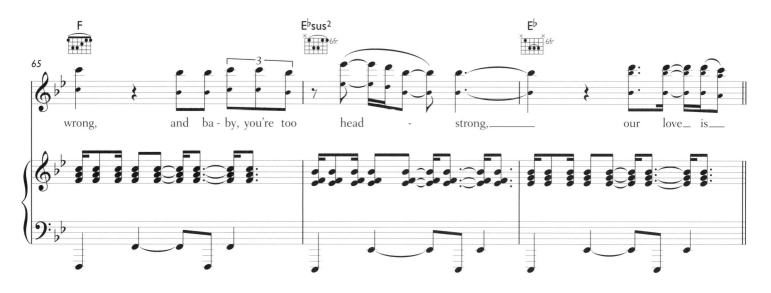

wrong,   and ba - by, you're too   head - strong,_____   our love_ is__

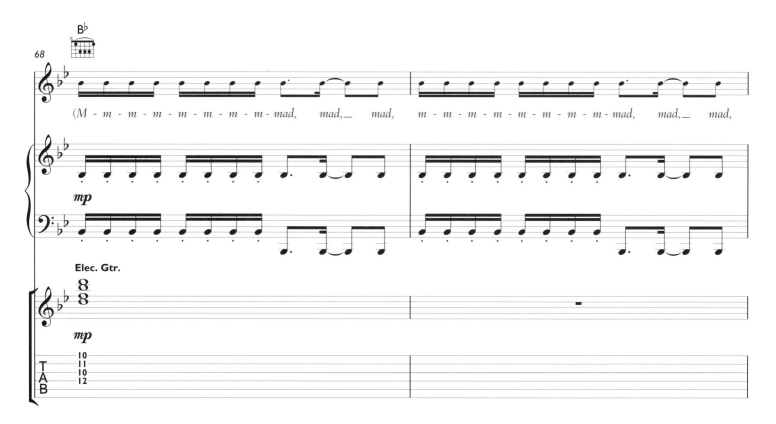

(M - m - m - m - m - m - m - m - mad, mad,_ mad,   m - m - m - m - m - m - m - m - mad, mad,_ mad,

Elec. Gtr.

m - m - m - m - m - m - m - m - mad, mad,_ mad,   m - m - m - m - m - m - m - m - mad - ness.)_

PANIC STATION

Words and Music by Matthew Bellamy

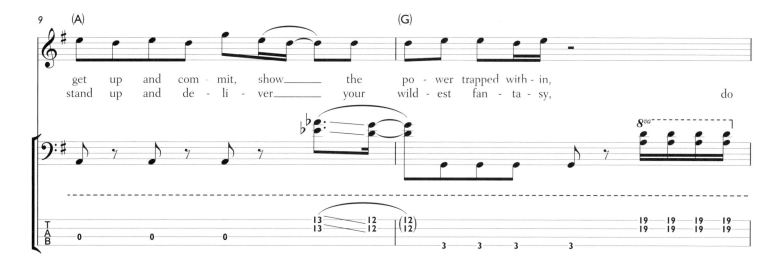

get up and com - mit, show_____ the po - wer trapped with - in,
stand up and de - li - ver_____ your wild - est fan - ta - sy, do

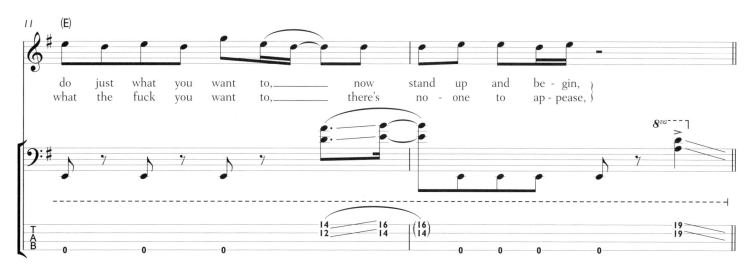

do just what you want to,_____ now stand up and be - gin,
what the fuck you want to,_____ there's no - one to ap - pease,

Ooh, 1, 2, 3, 4, fi - re's in your eyes,_____ and this cha-

Electric Guitar
with crunch

(Bass)
with crunch
Fig. 3

Synth. *(2° only)*

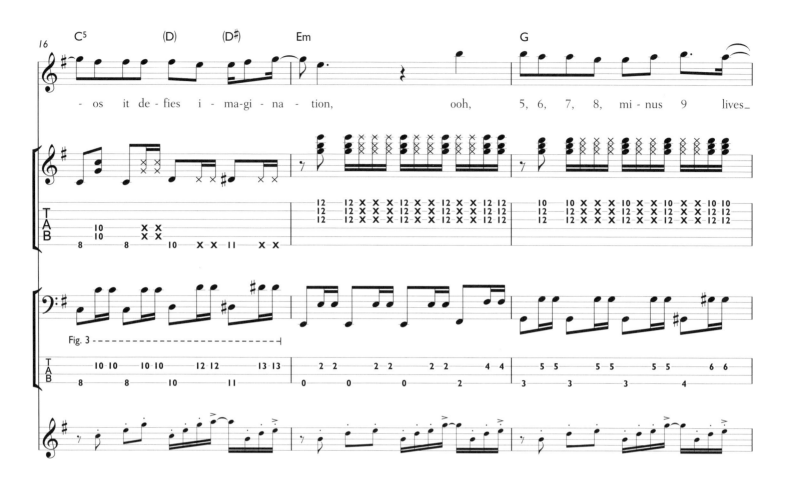

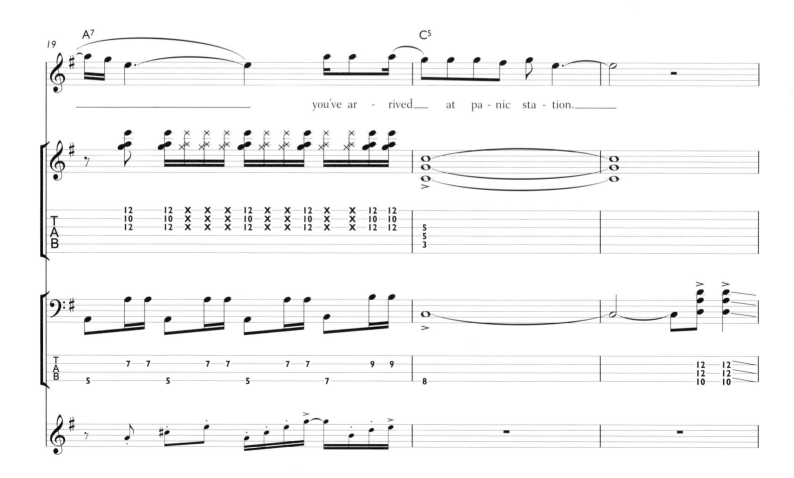

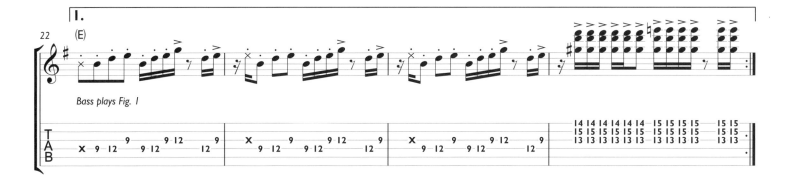

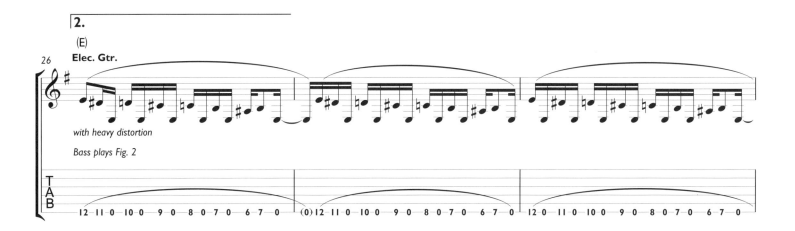

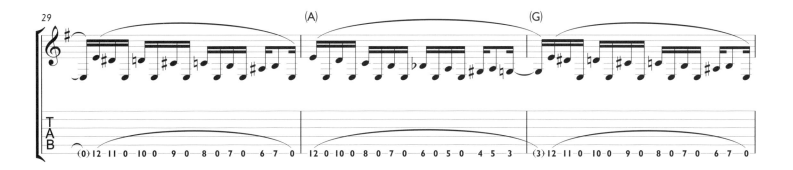

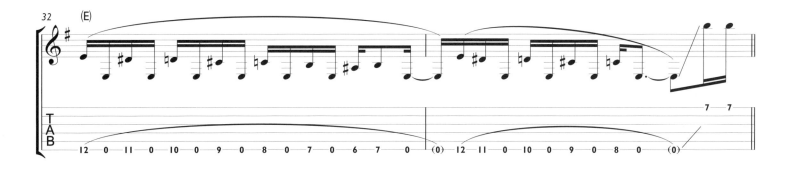

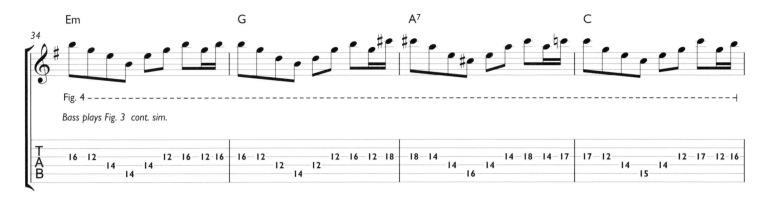

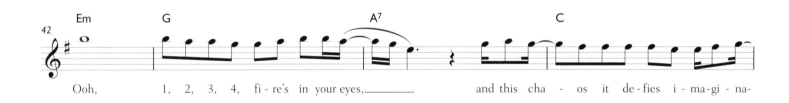

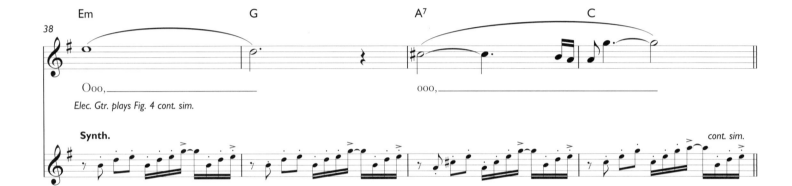

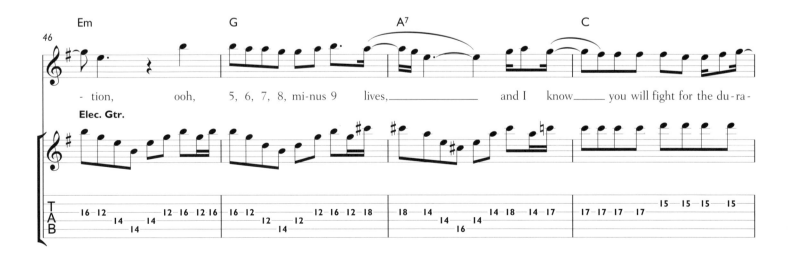

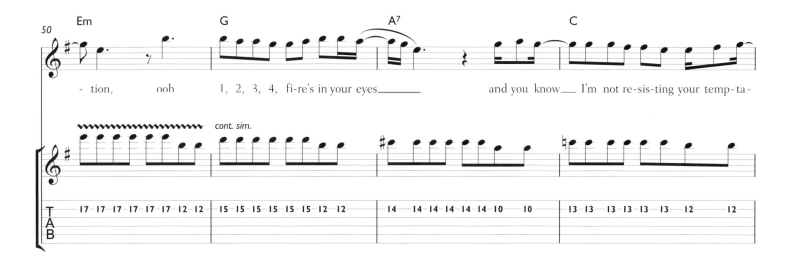

- tion, ooh 1, 2, 3, 4, fi-re's in your eyes_____ and you know___ I'm not re-sis-ting your temp-ta-

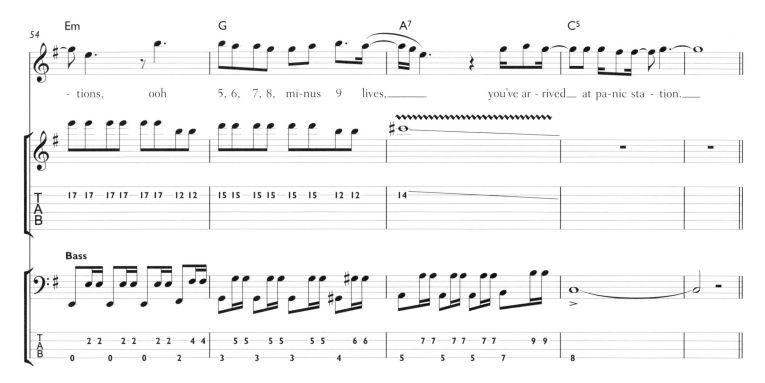

- tions, ooh 5, 6, 7, 8, mi-nus 9 lives,_____ you've ar-rived___ at pa-nic sta - tion.___

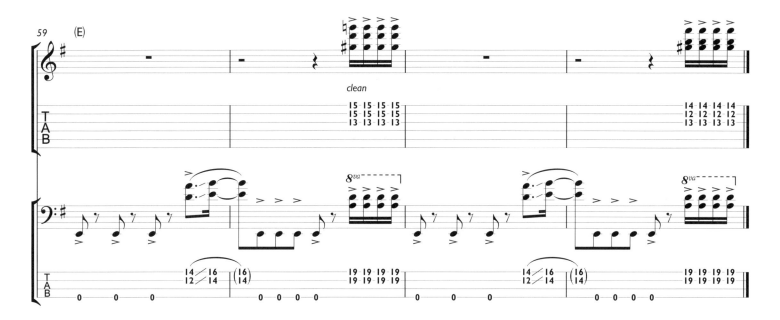

PRELUDE

Words and Music by Matthew Bellamy

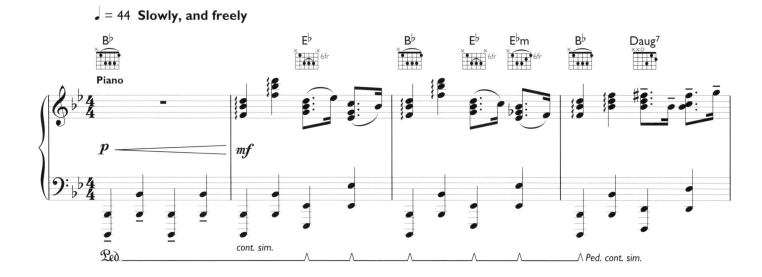

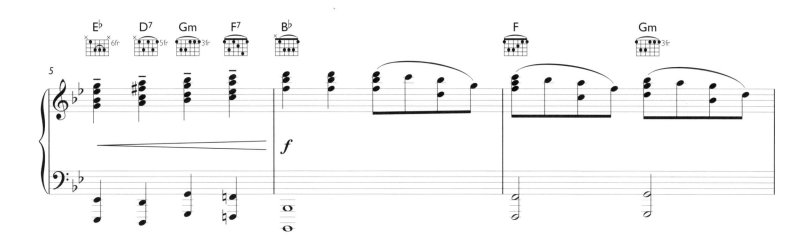

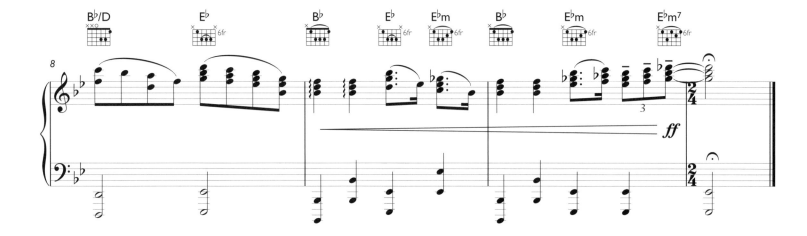

SURVIVAL

Words and Music by Matthew Bellamy

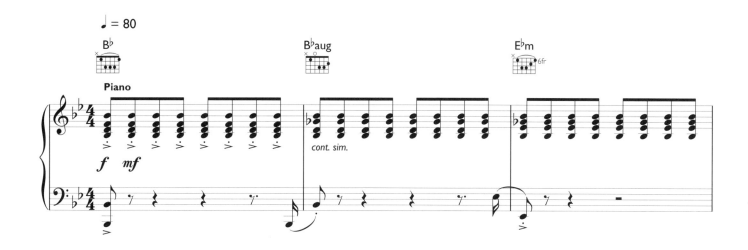

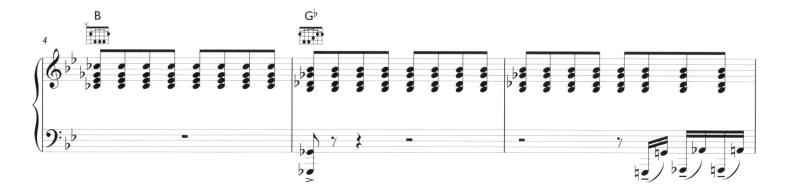

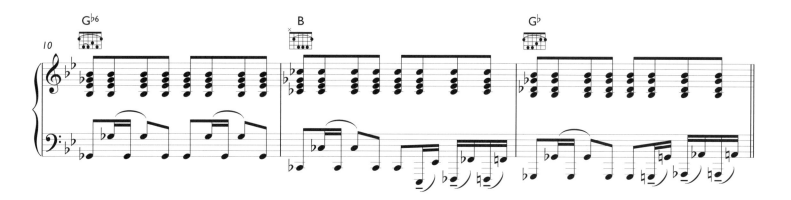

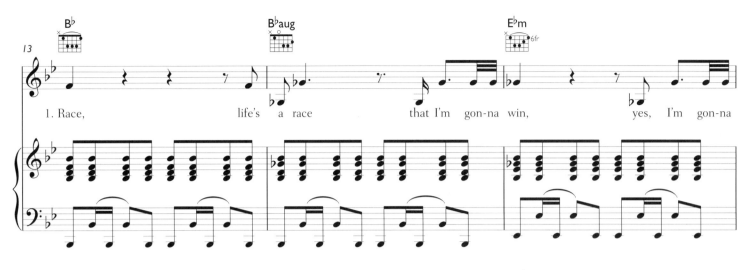

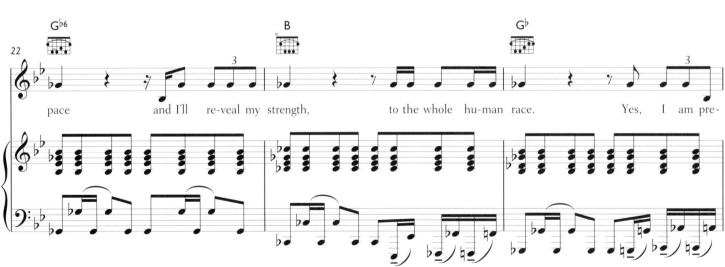

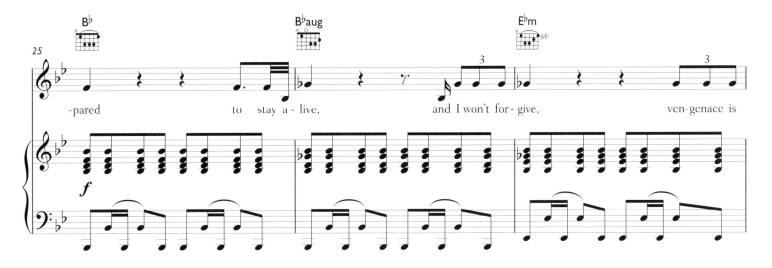

-pared   to   stay a - live,   and I won't for - give,   ven-genace is

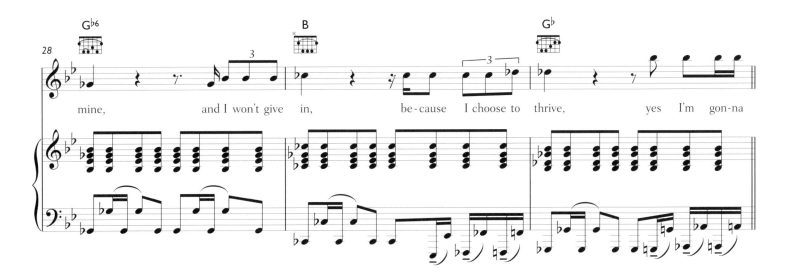

mine,   and I won't give   in,   be-cause   I choose to   thrive,   yes I'm gon-na

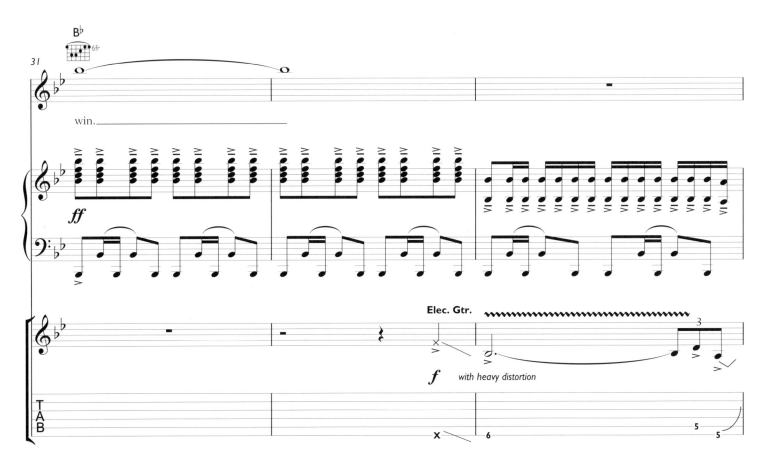

win.

Elec. Gtr.

f *with heavy distortion*

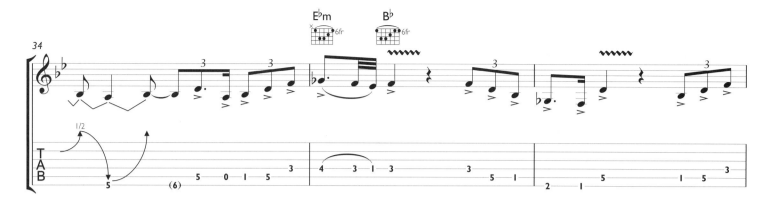

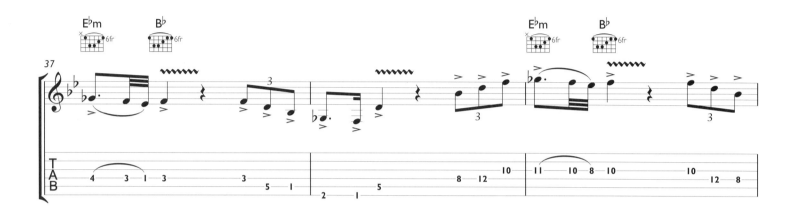

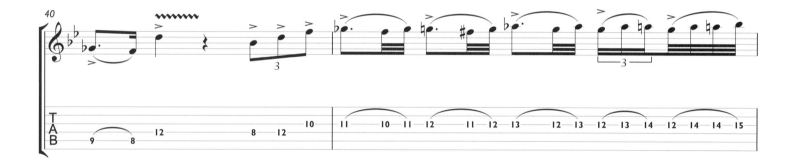

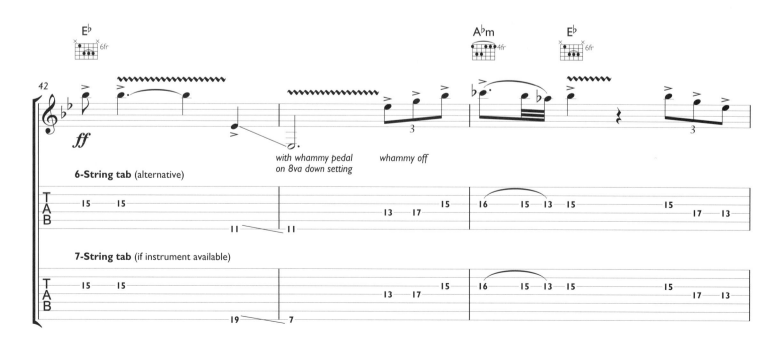

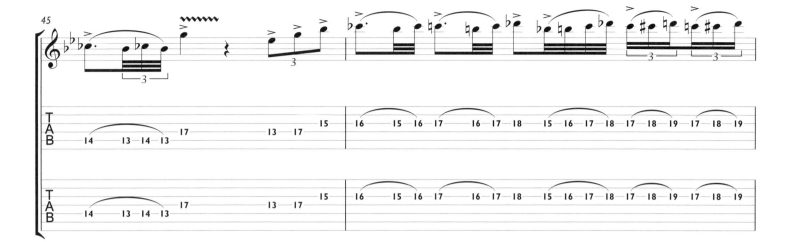

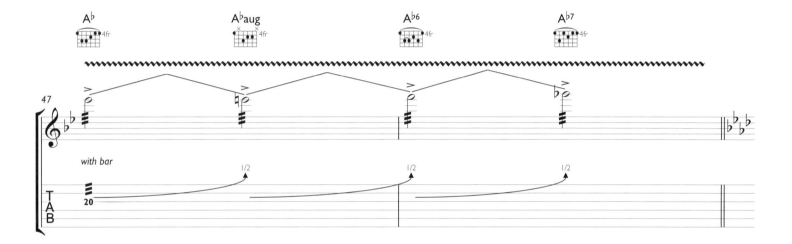

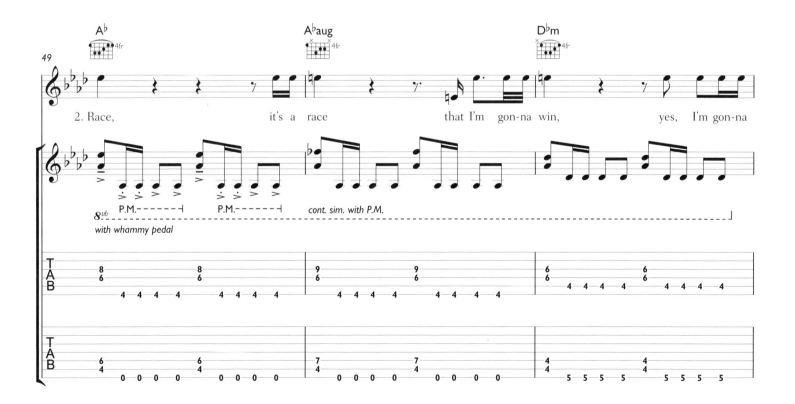

2. Race,   it's a race   that I'm gon-na win,   yes, I'm gon-na

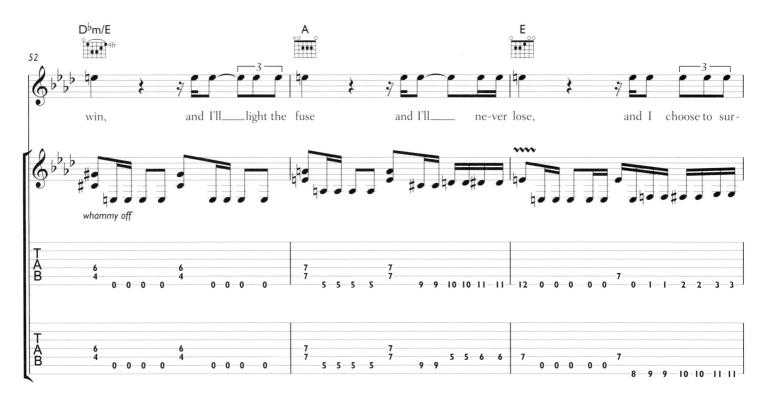

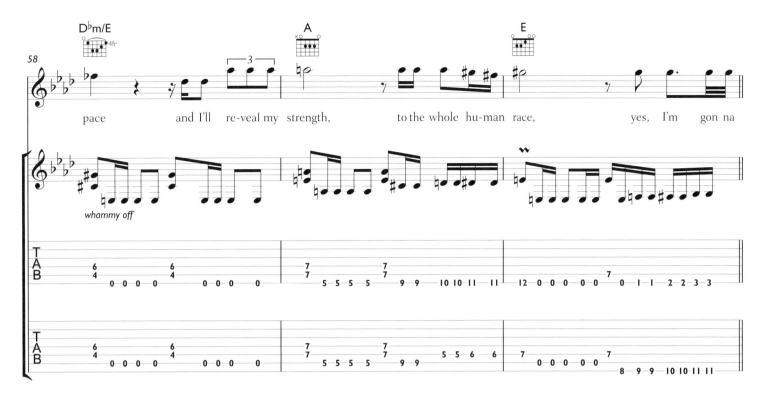

pace   and I'll   re-veal my   strength,   to the whole hu-man race,   yes,   I'm   gon-na

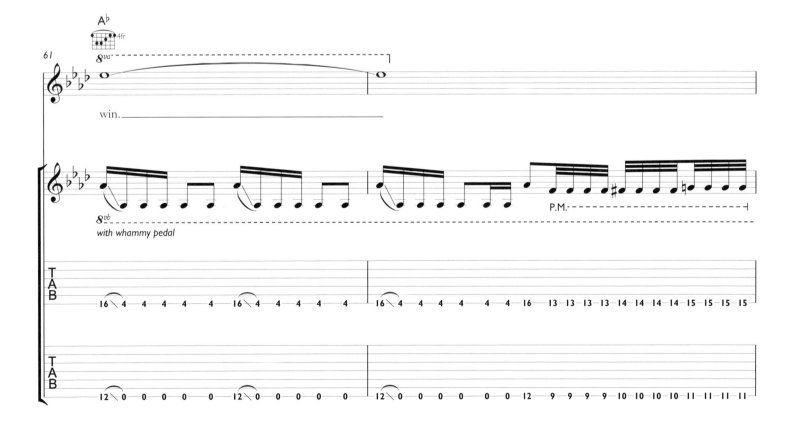

win.

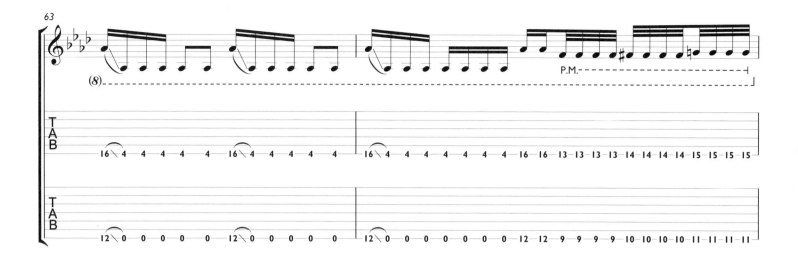

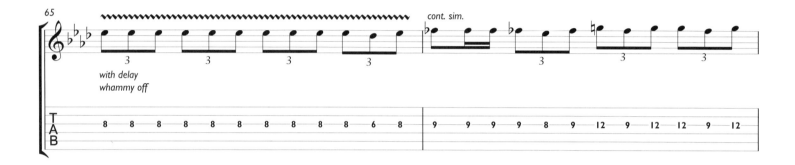

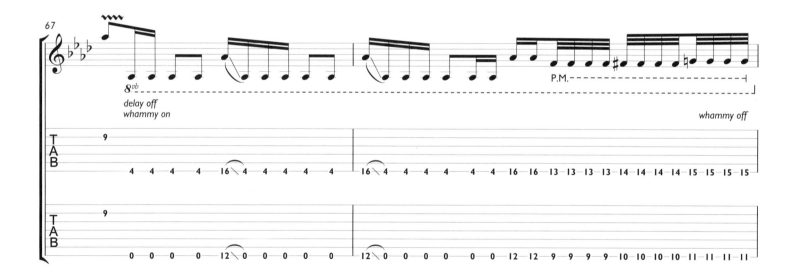

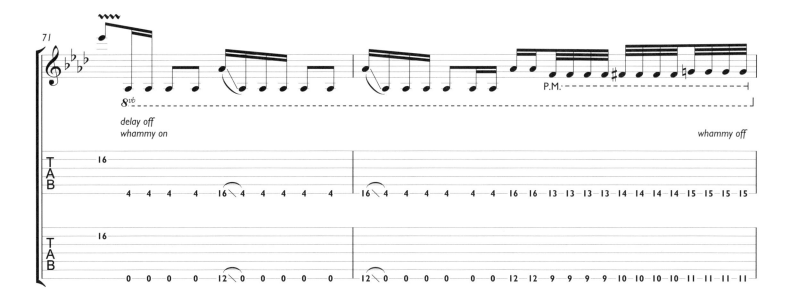

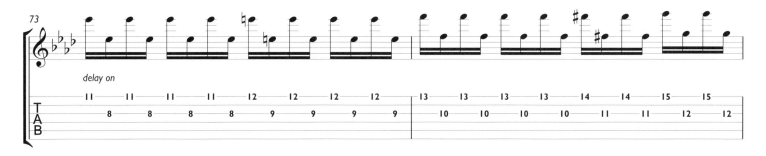

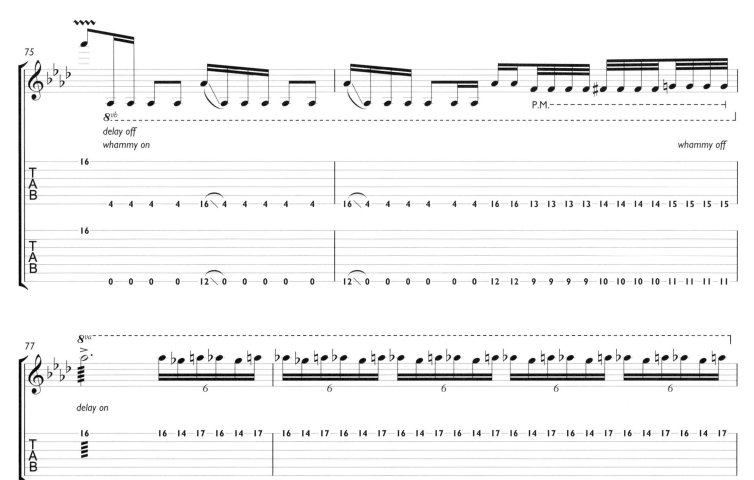

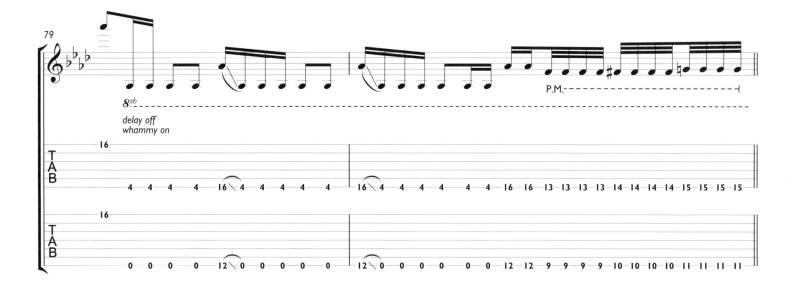

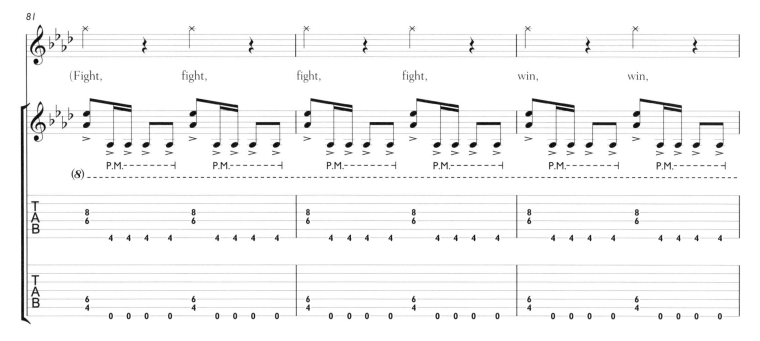

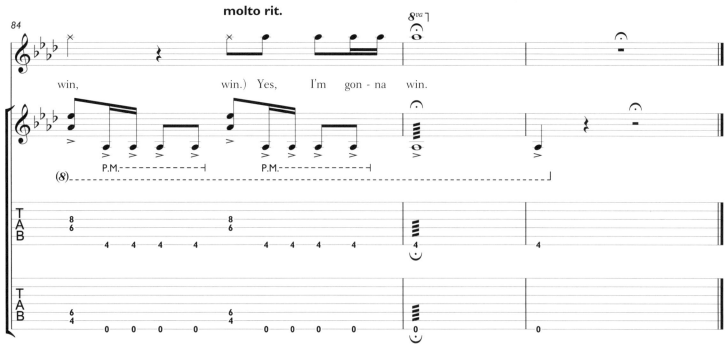

FOLLOW ME

Words and Music by Matthew Bellamy

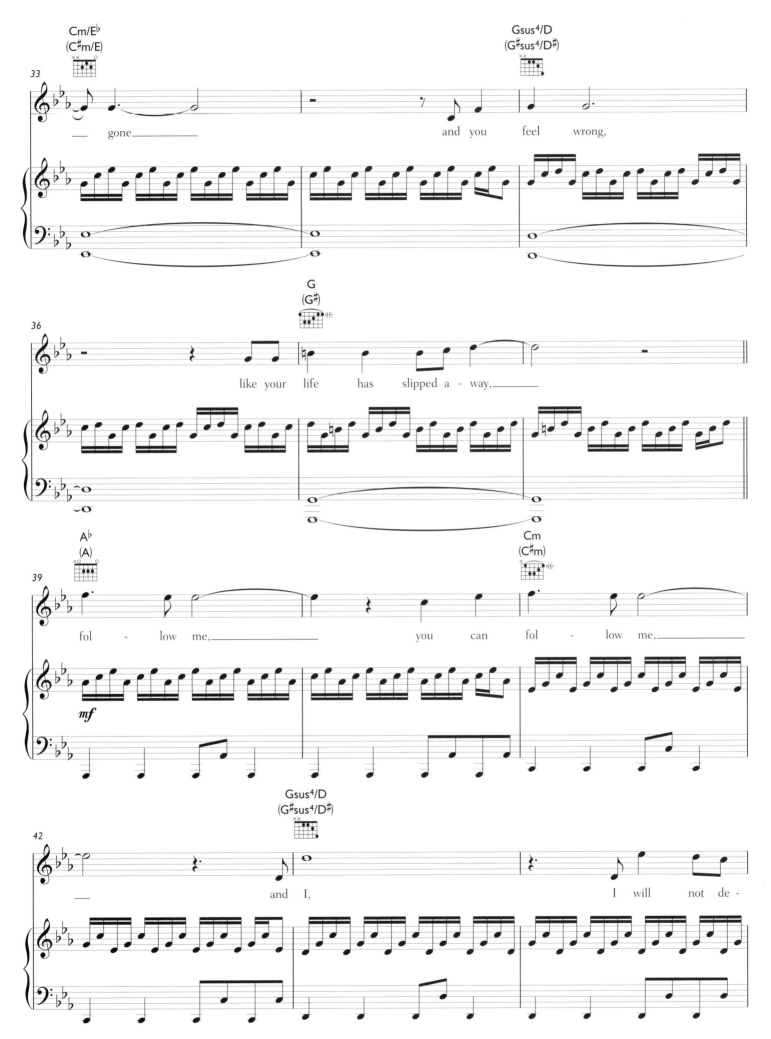

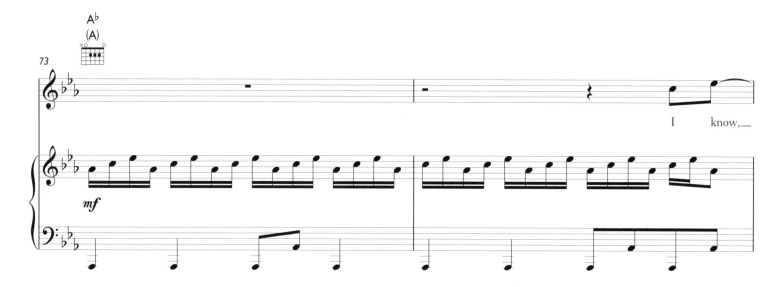

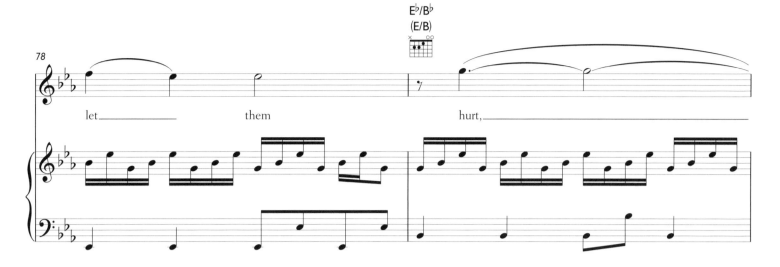

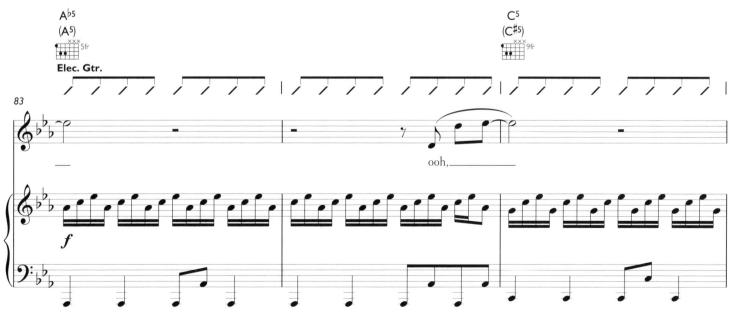

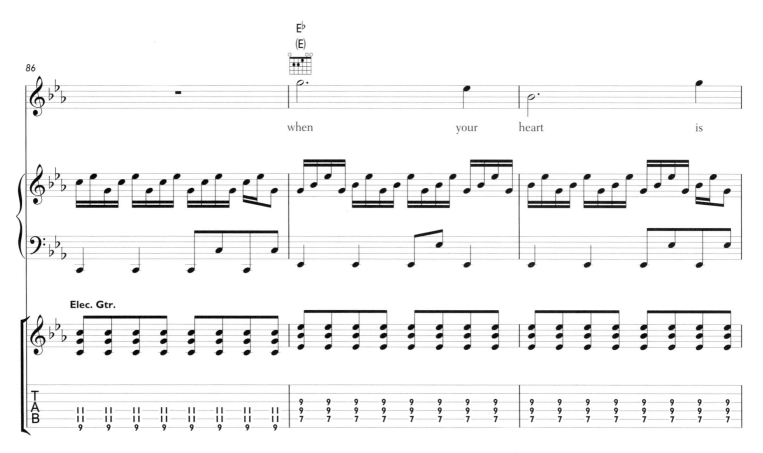

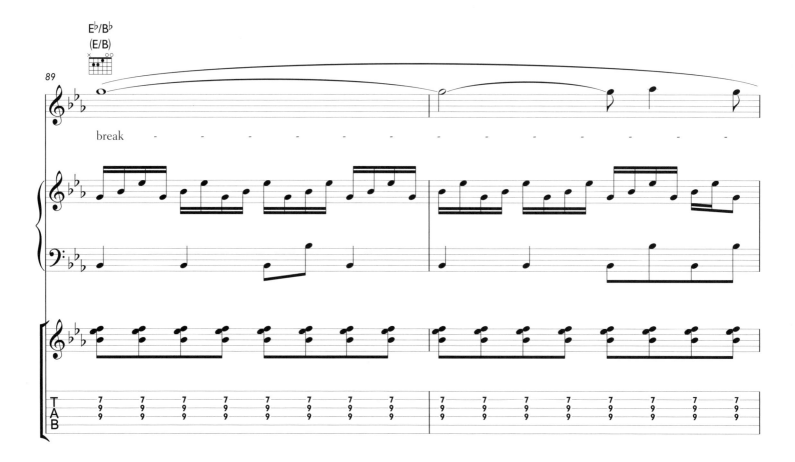

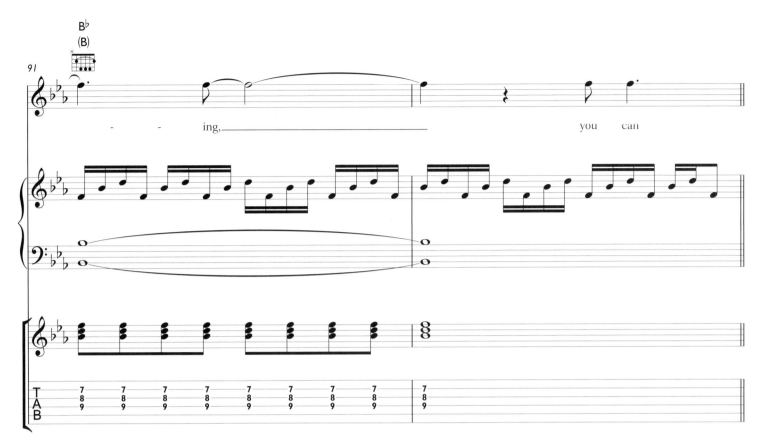

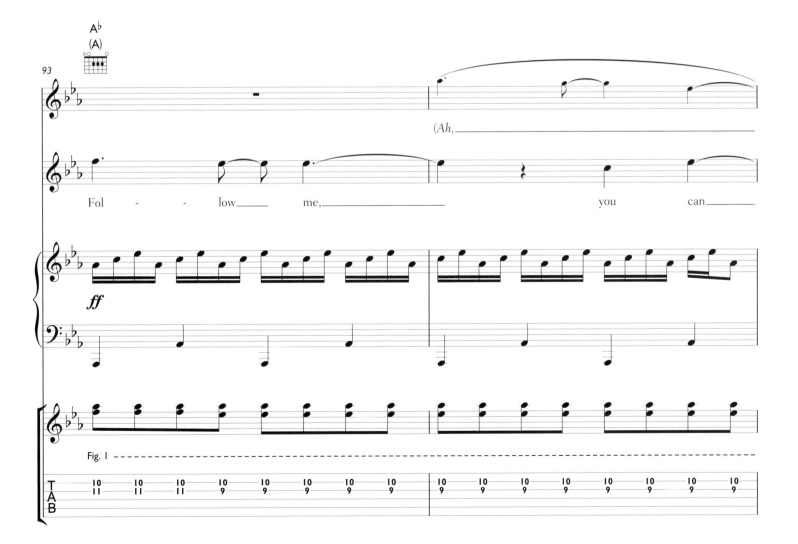

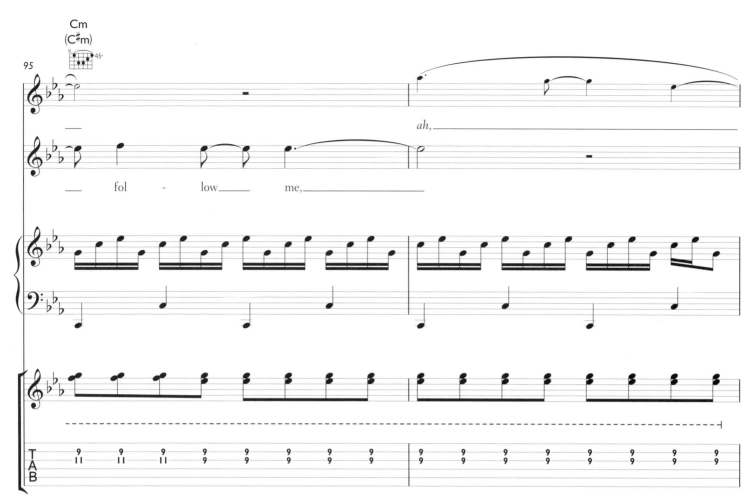

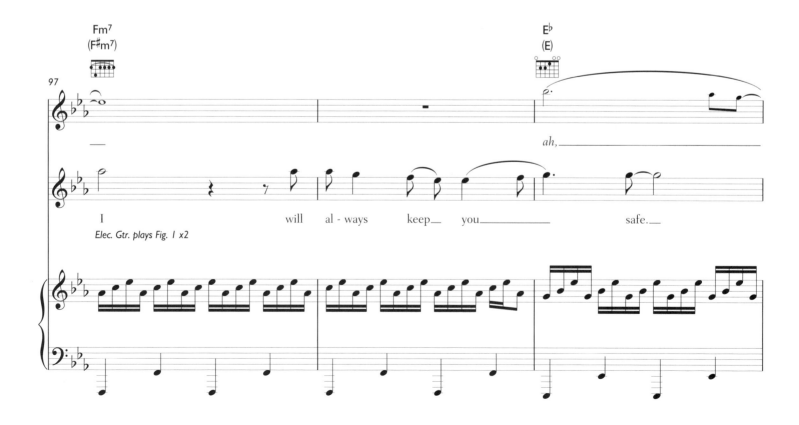

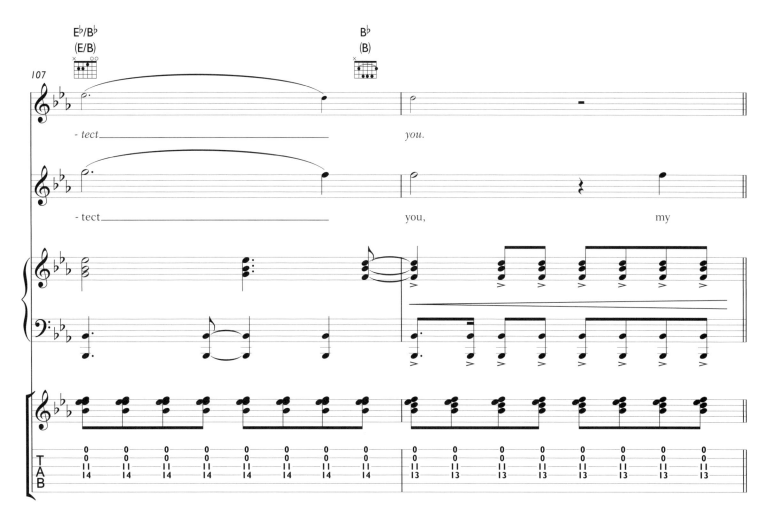

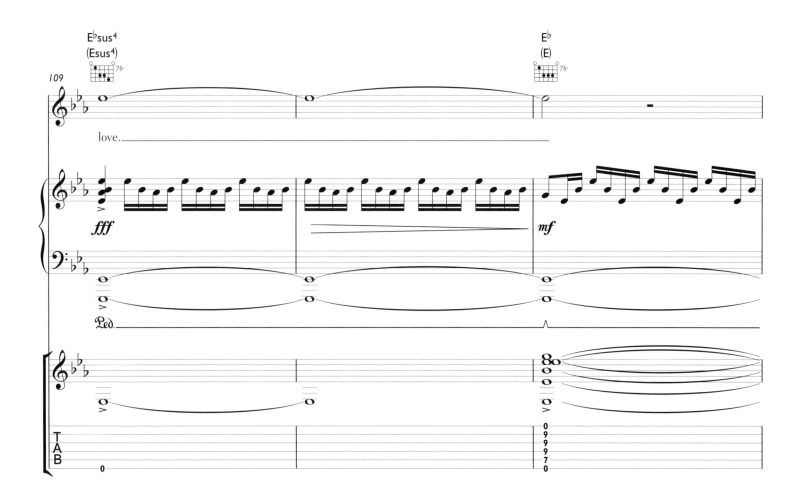

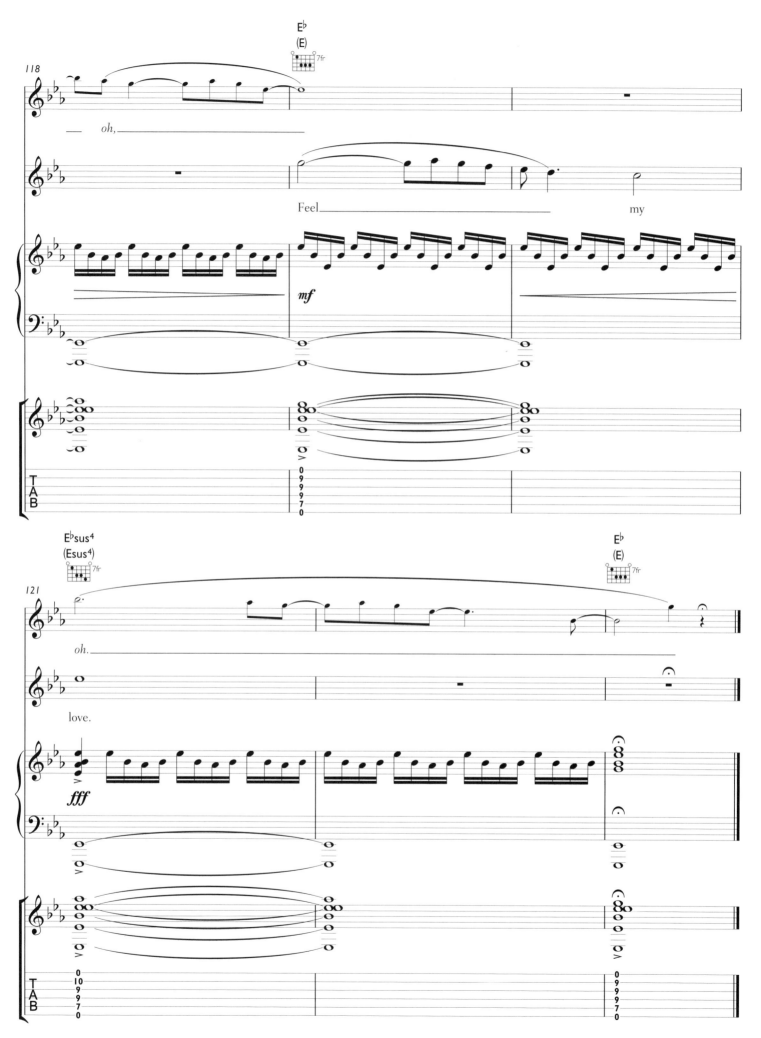

ANIMALS

Words and Music by Matthew Bellamy

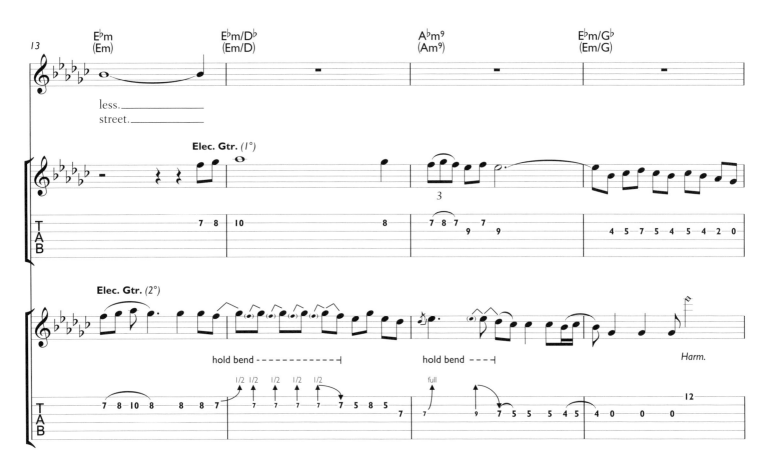

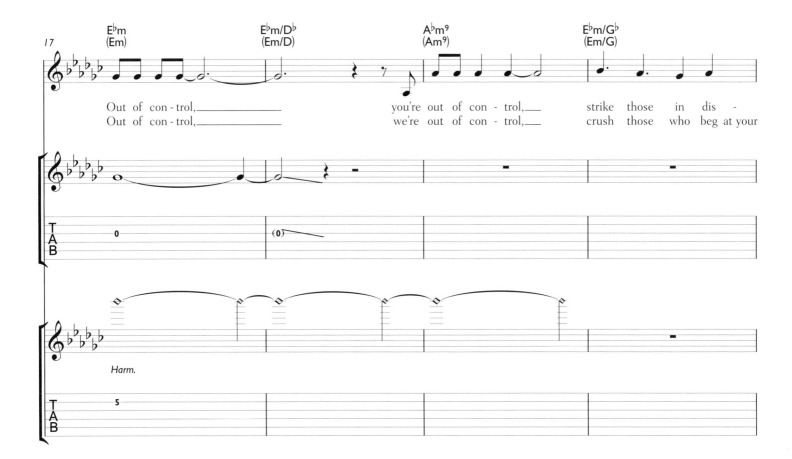

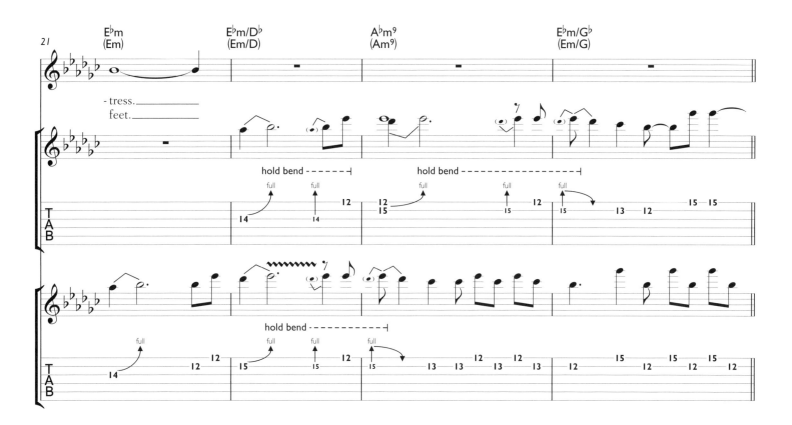

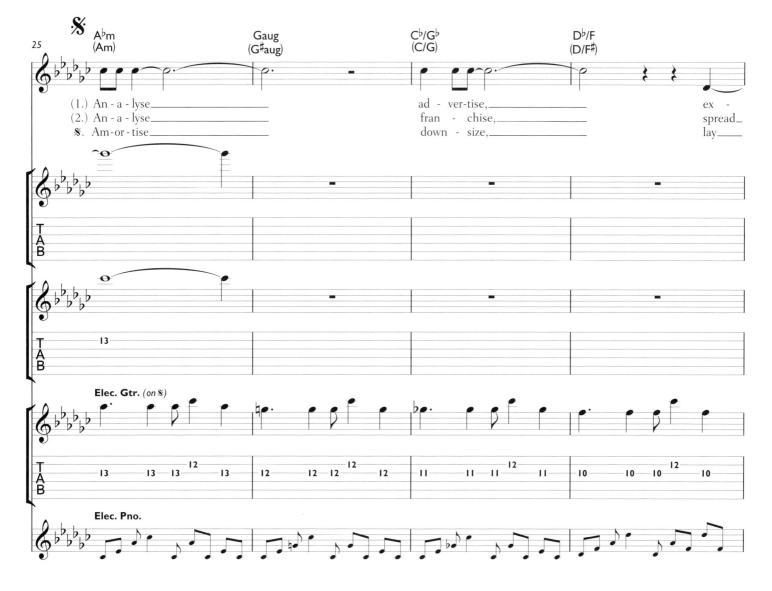

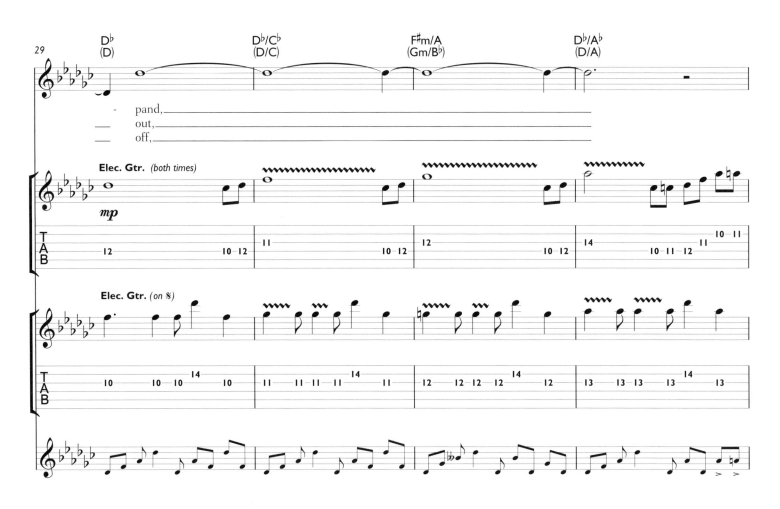

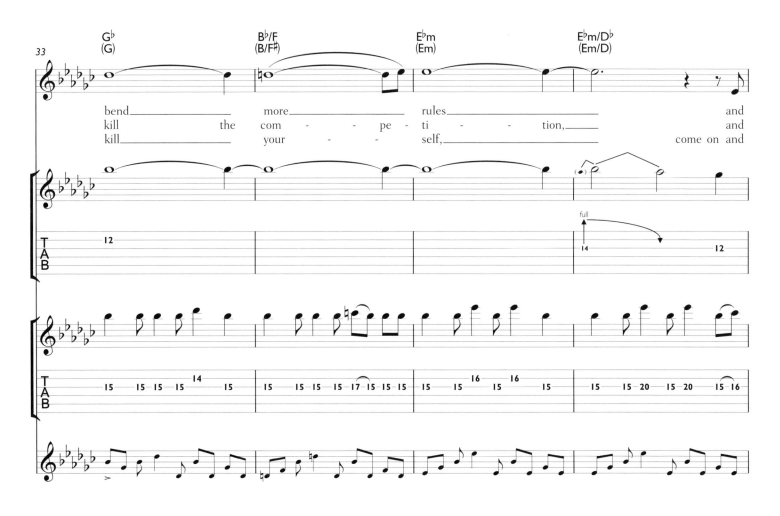

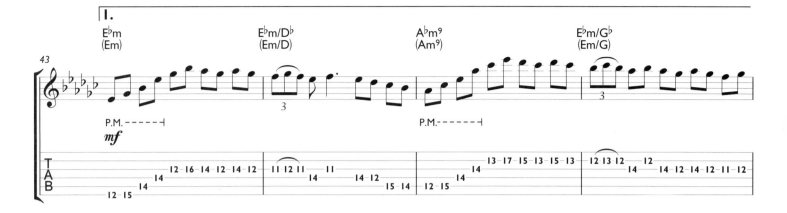

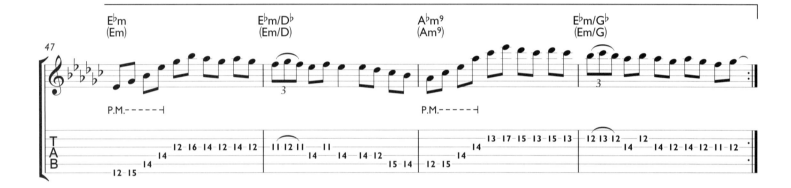

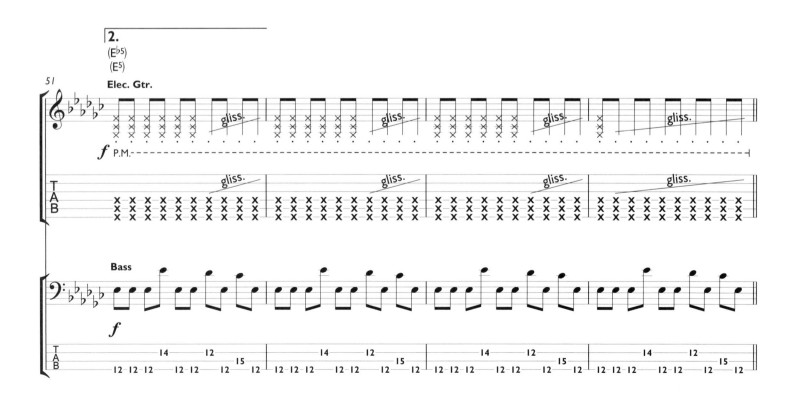

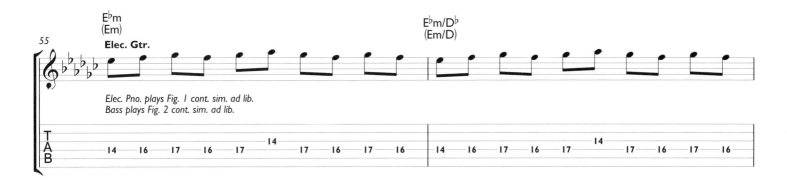

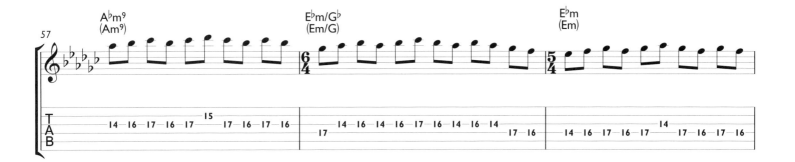

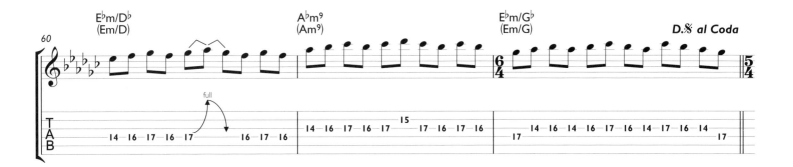

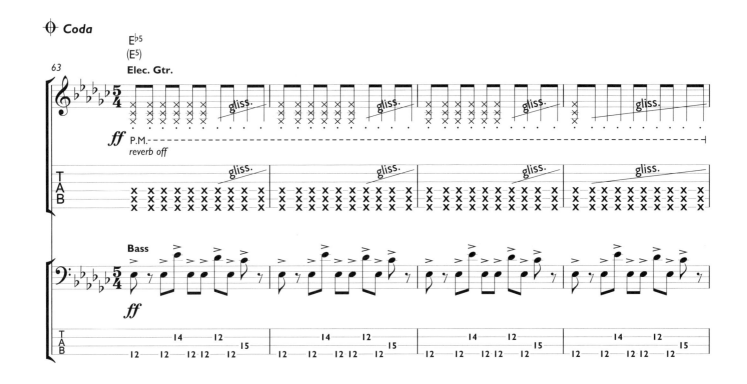

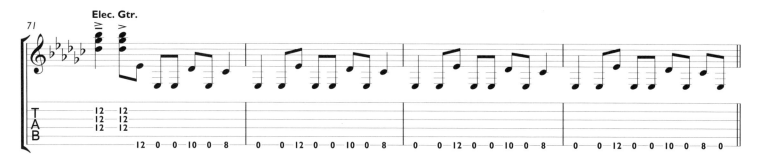

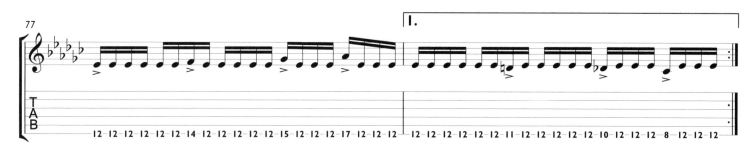

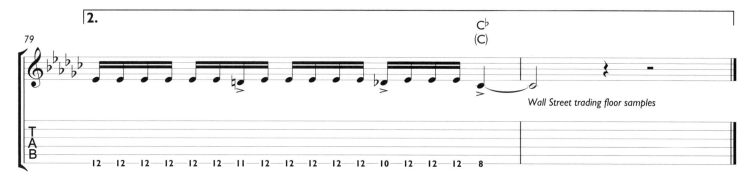

EXPLORERS

Words and Music by Matthew Bellamy

1. Once I hoped to seek the new and un - known,_ this
(2.) world lush and blue, with riv - ers run - ning_ wild,_ they'll

plan - et's o - ver - run, there's noth - ing left_ for you or_ for me.
be re - rout - ed south, with none_ left_ for you or_ for me.

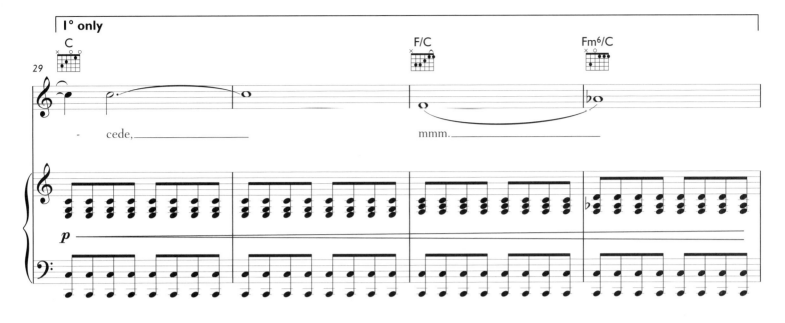

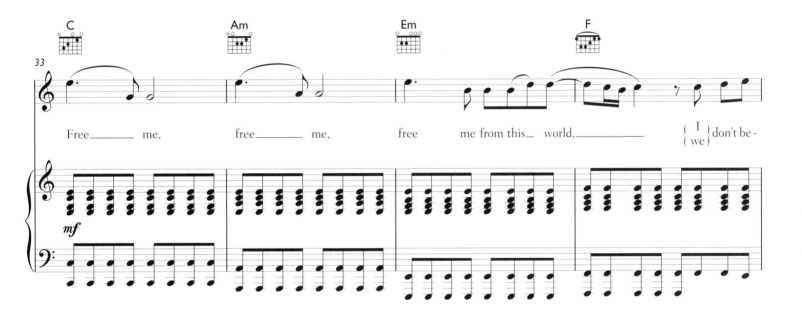

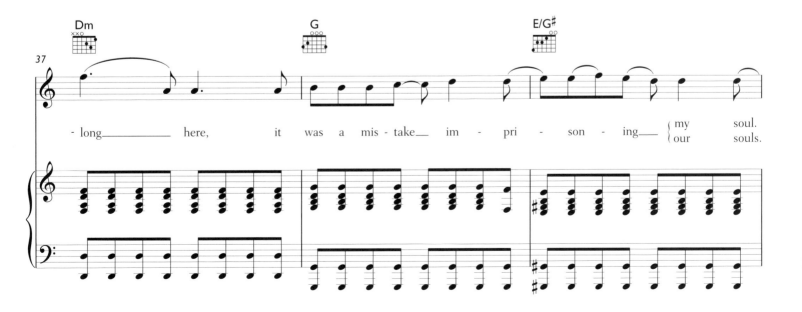

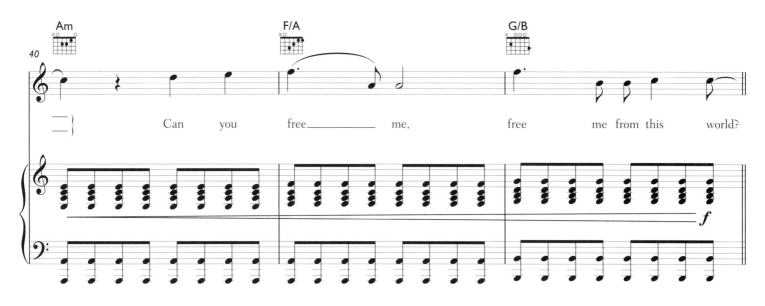

Can you free_____ me, free me from this world?

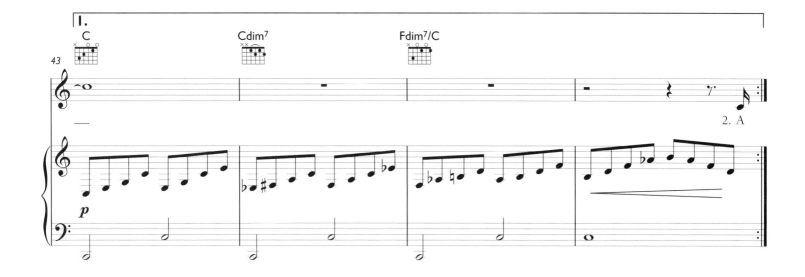

2. A

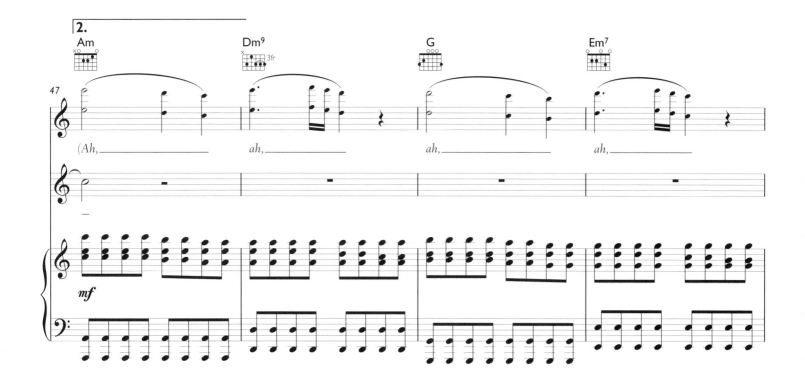

(Ah,_____ ah,_____ ah,_____ ah,_____

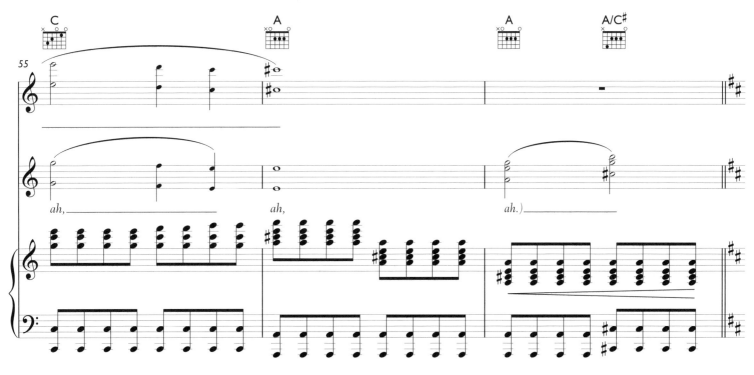

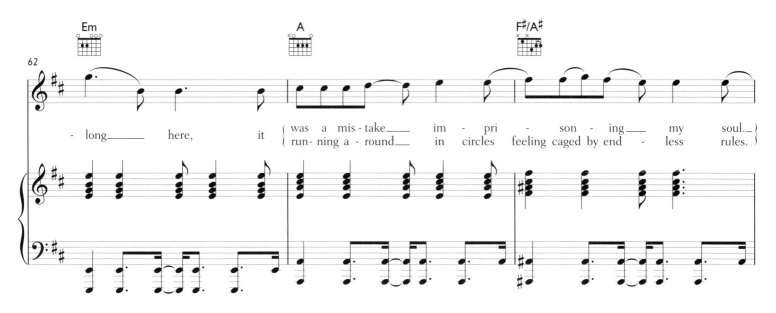

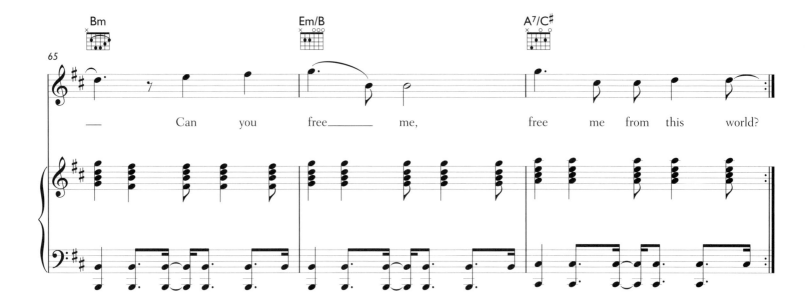

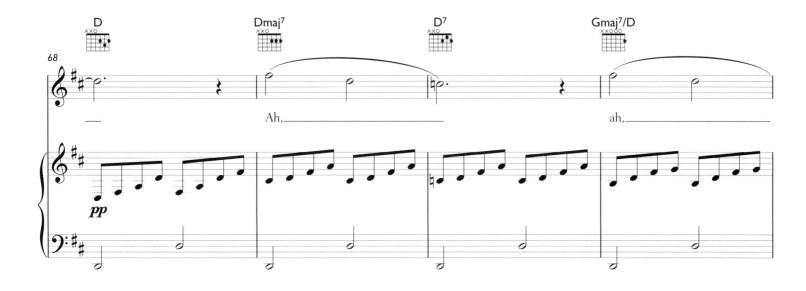

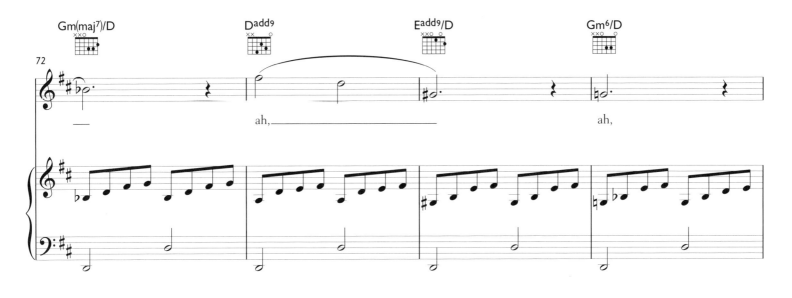

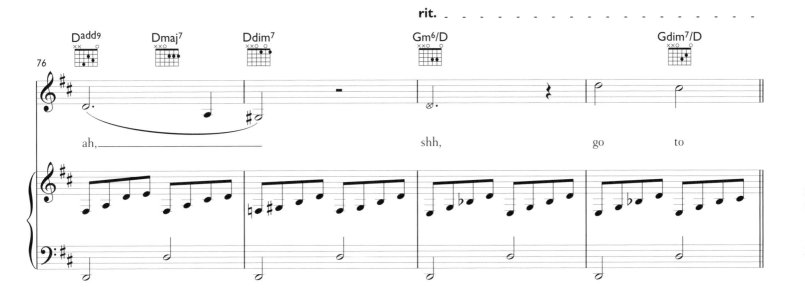

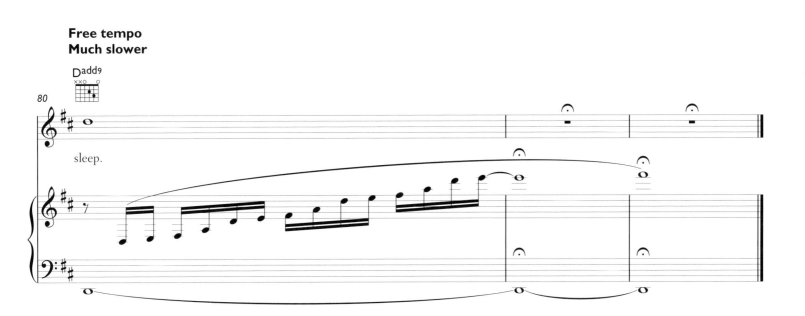

BIG FREEZE

Words and Music by Matthew Bellamy

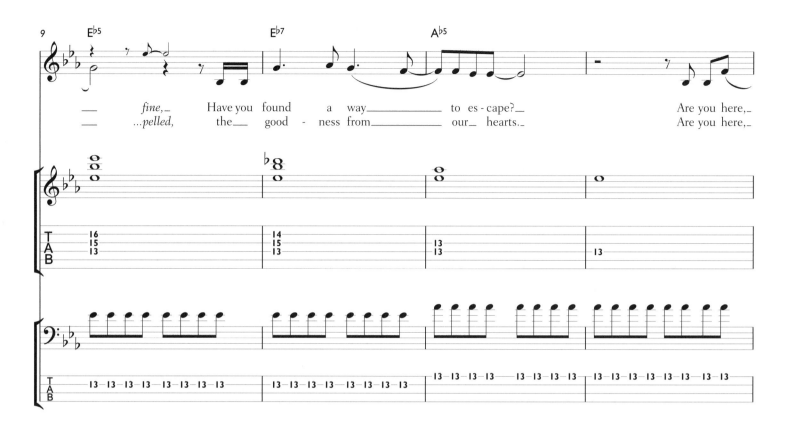

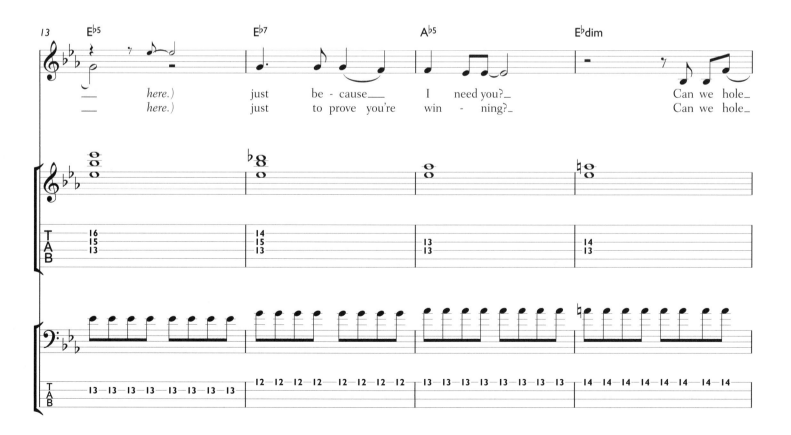

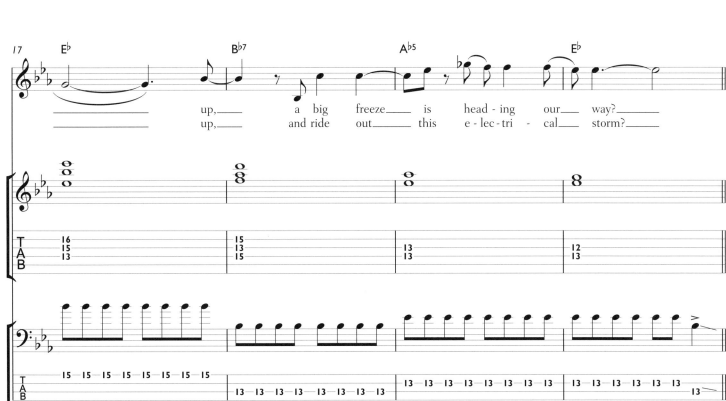

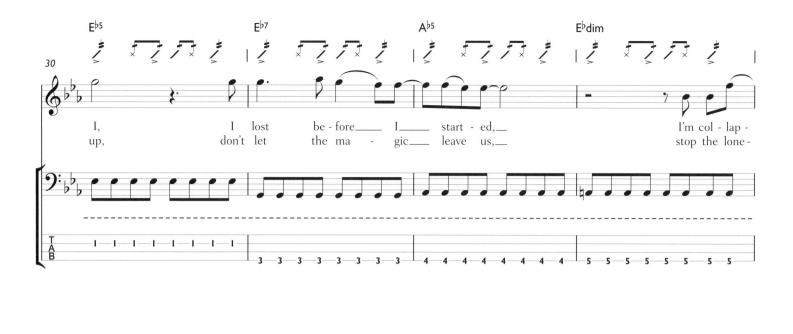

I, I lost be - fore____ I____ start - ed,____ I'm col - lap -
up, don't let the ma - gic____ leave us,____ stop the lone -

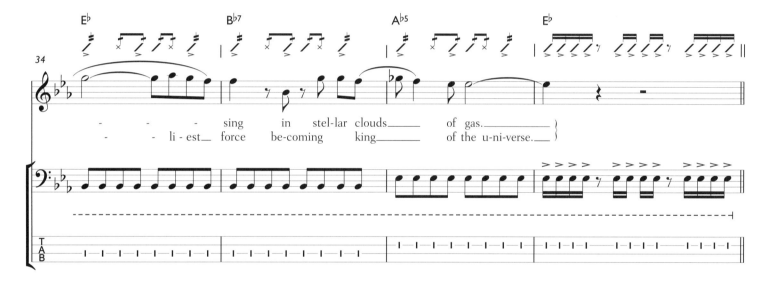

- - - - sing in stel - lar clouds____ of gas.____
- - li - est____ force be - coming king____ of the u - ni - verse.____

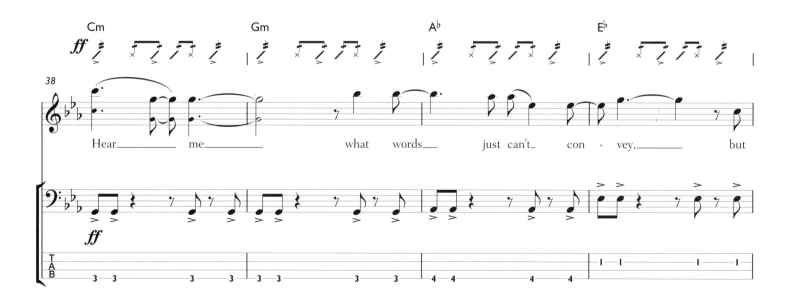

Hear_____ me_____ what words____ just can't_ con - vey,____ but

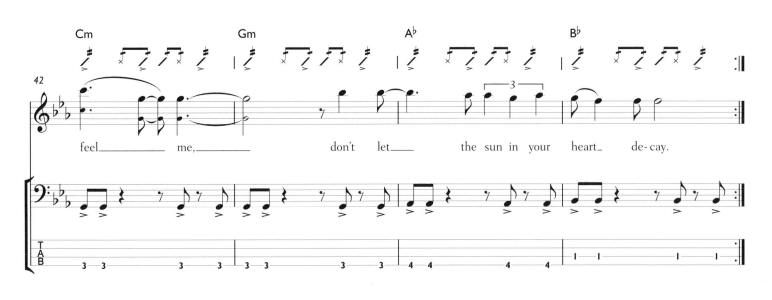

feel_____ me,_____ don't let____ the sun in your heart_ de-cay.

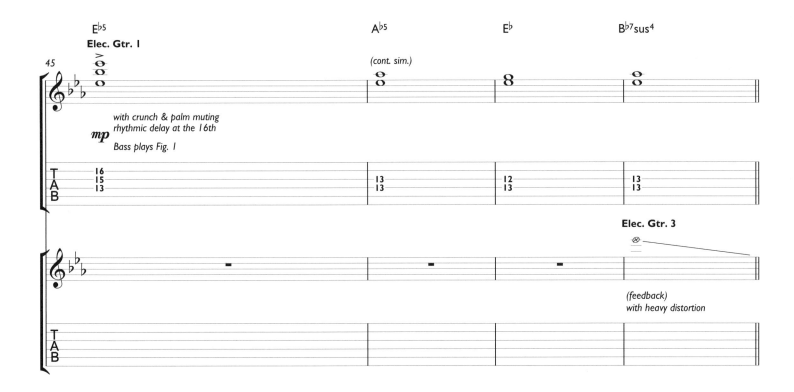

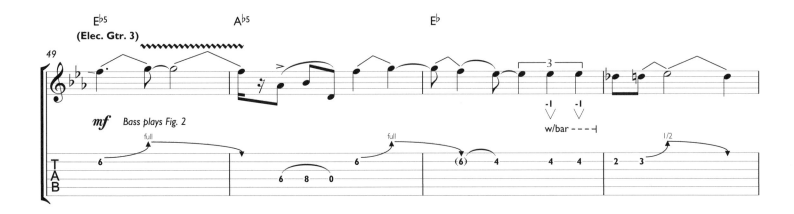

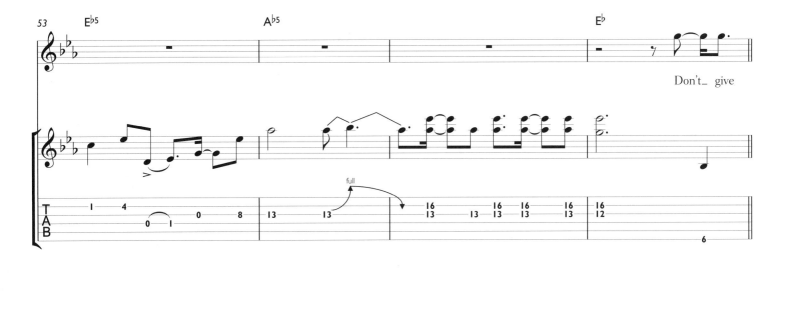

Don't_ give

up, don't let the ma - gic____ leave_ us,____ we're col - lap-

- - sing in stel - lar clouds____ of_ gas____ yeah.____

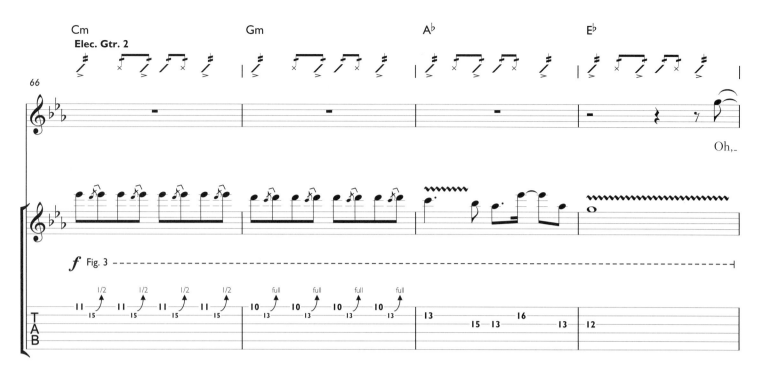

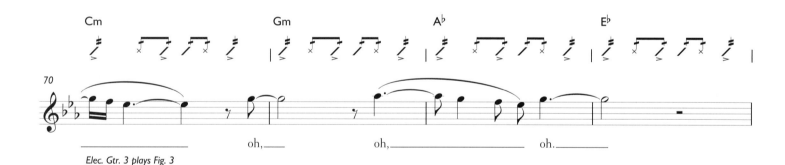

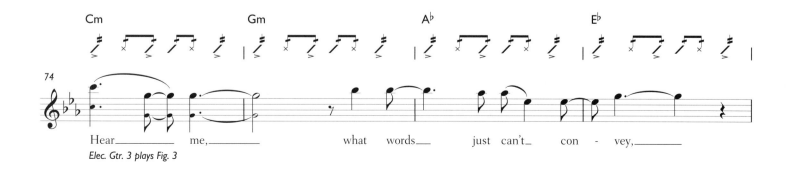

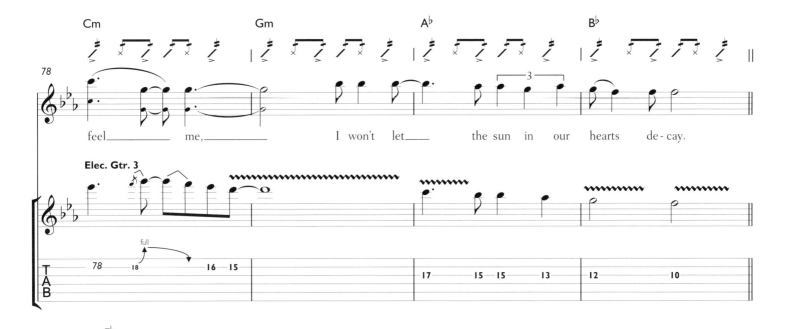

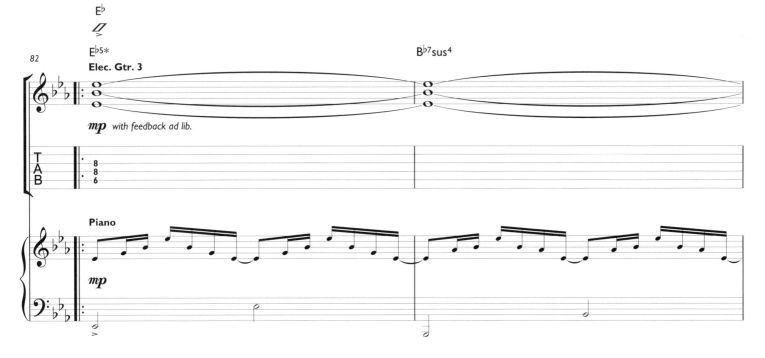

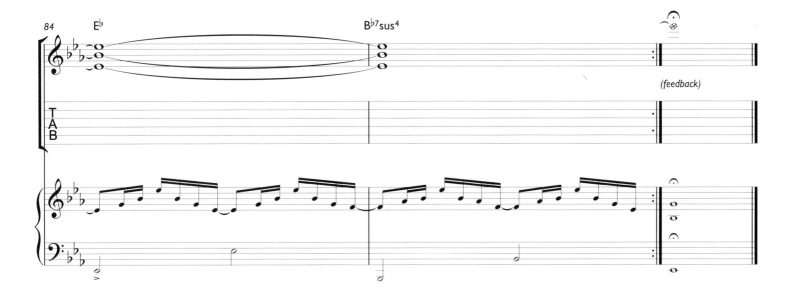

SAVE ME

Words and Music by Chris Wolstenholme

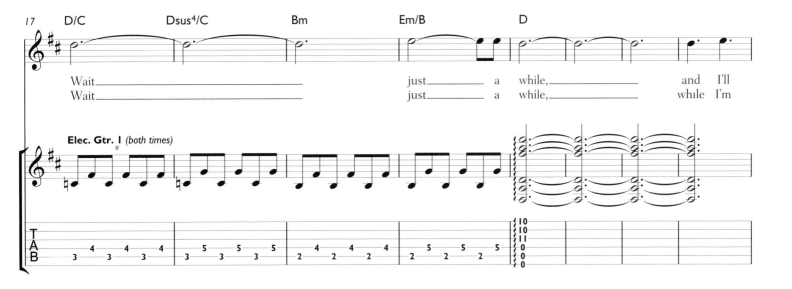

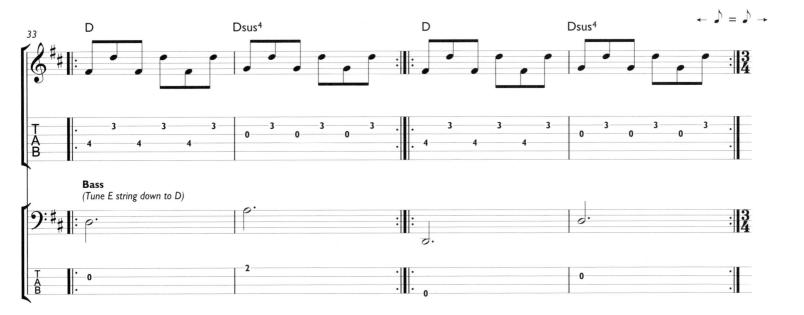

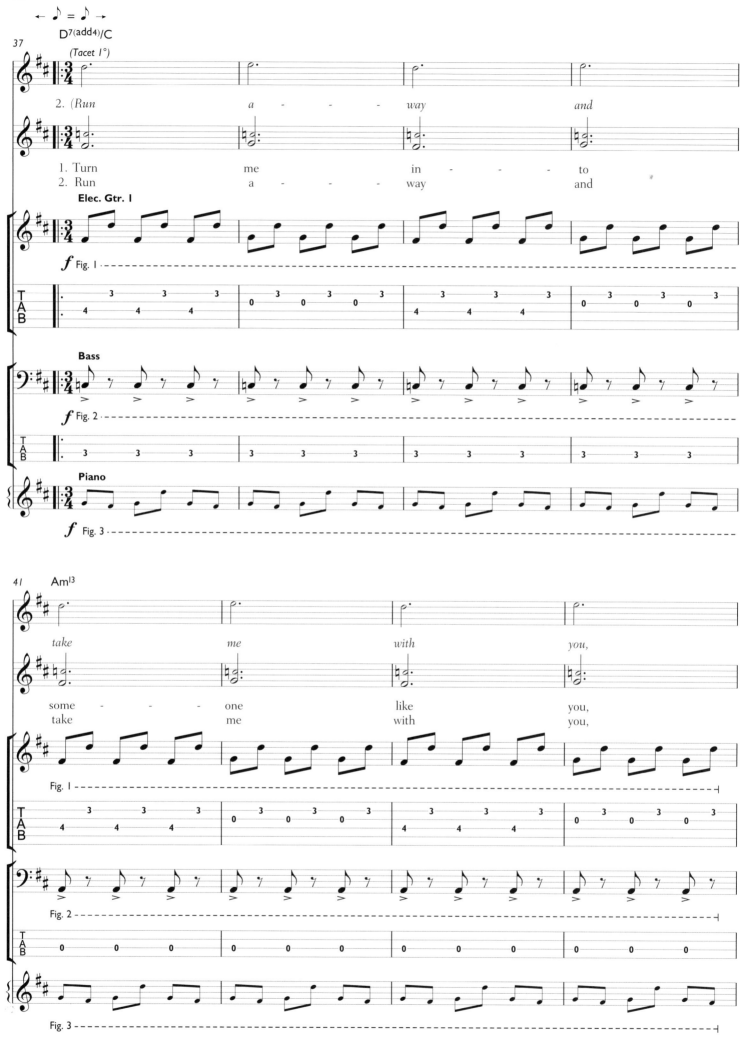

don't let go I need your res - cue.

find a place that we can go to,
don't let go I need your res - cue.

Elec. Gtr. 1 plays Fig. 1
Bass plays Fig. 2
Piano plays Fig. 3

Watch___ me,___ cause I'm on a mis - sion,

hold me back, so I'm forced to___ lis - ten.

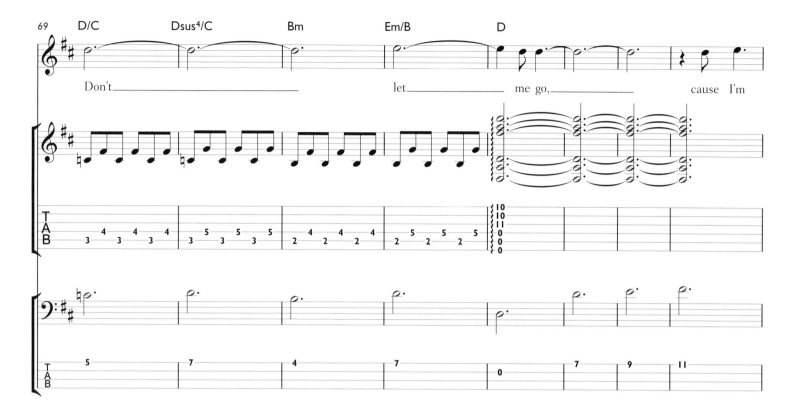

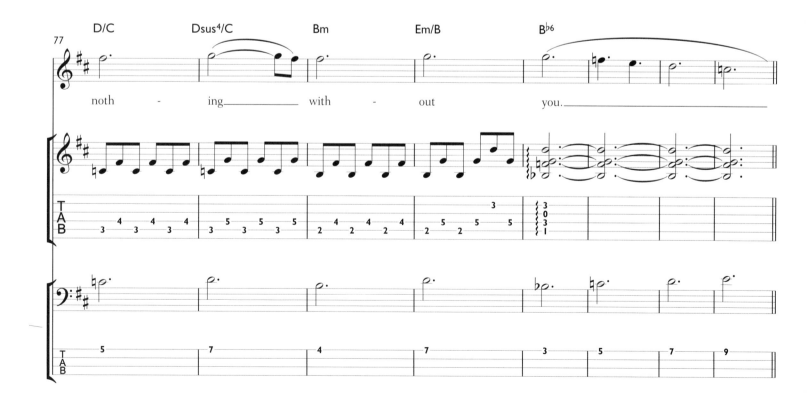

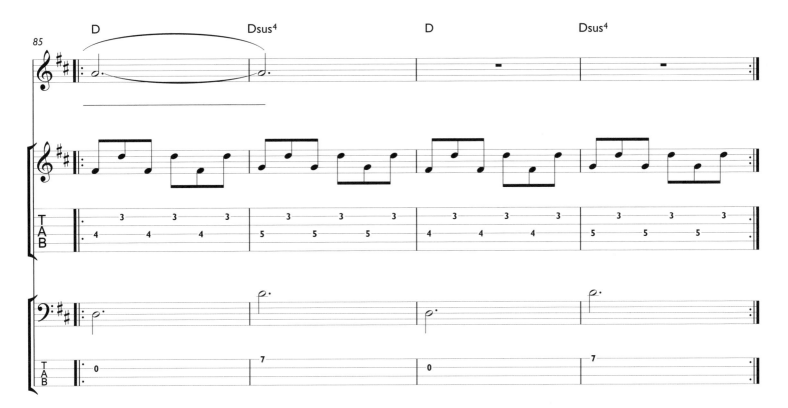

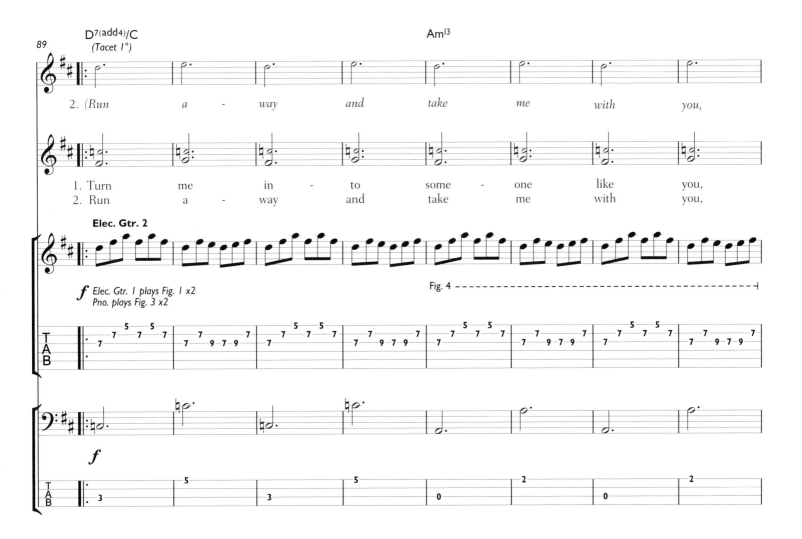

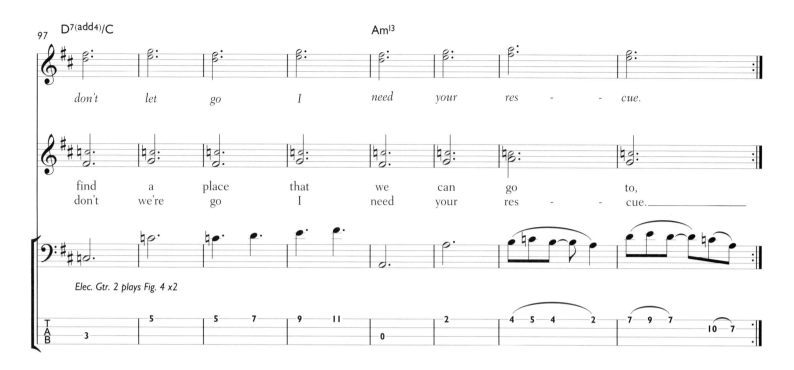

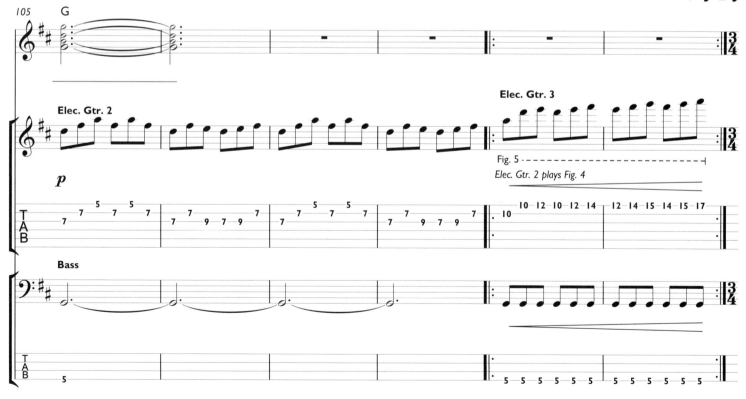

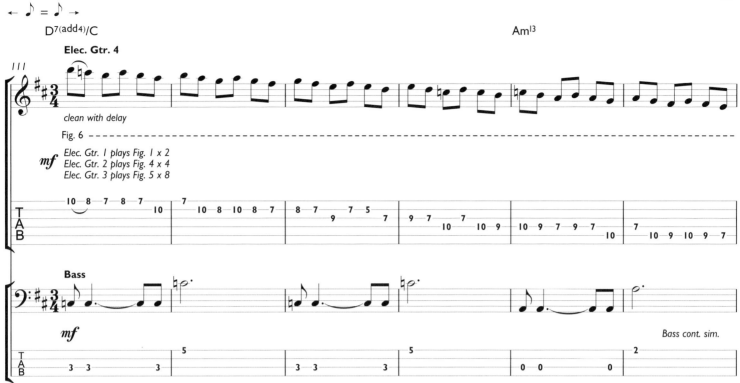

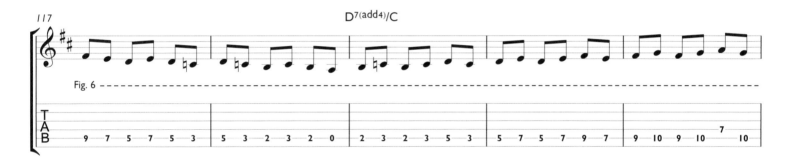

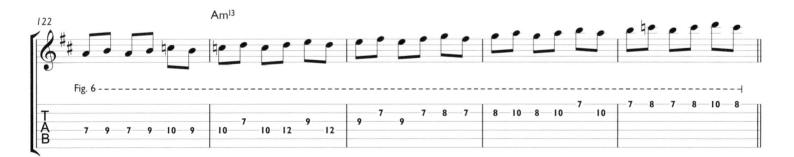

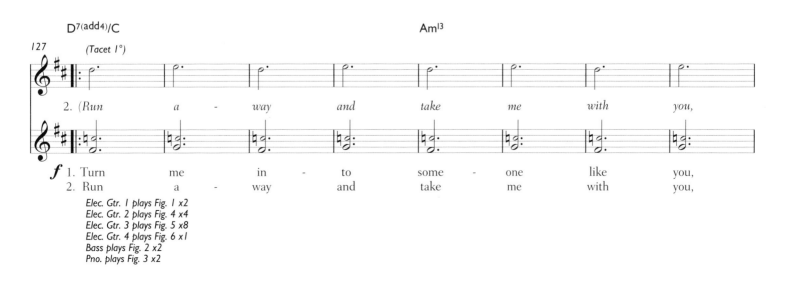

LIQUID STATE

Words and Music by Chris Wolstenholme

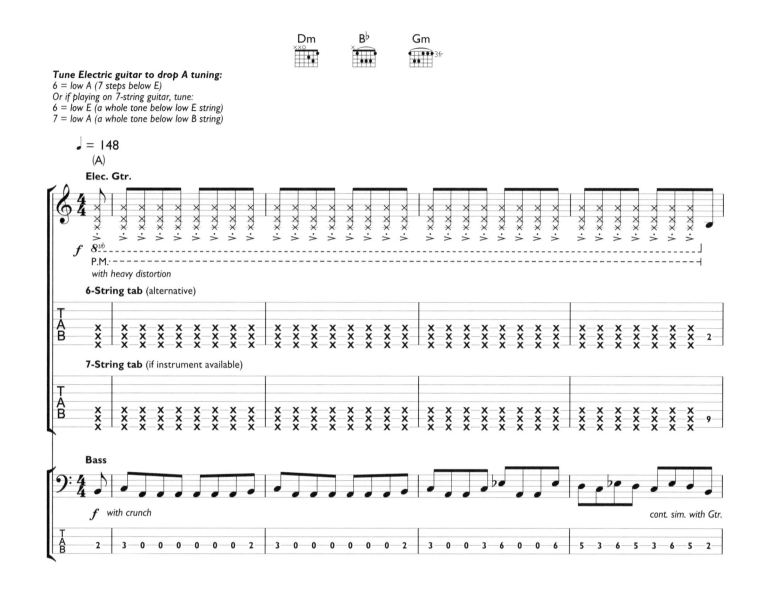

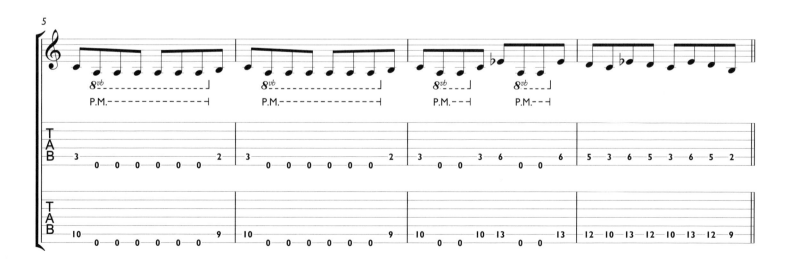

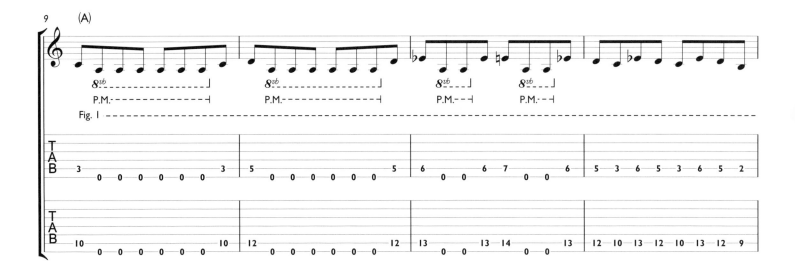

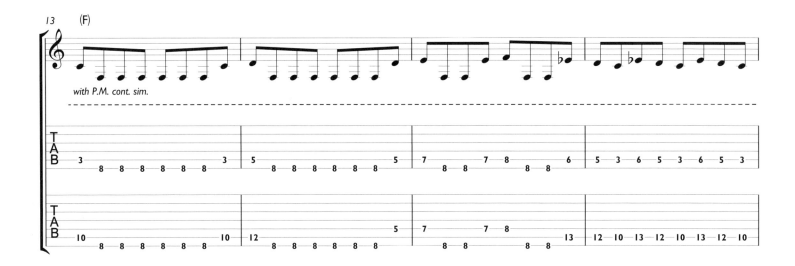

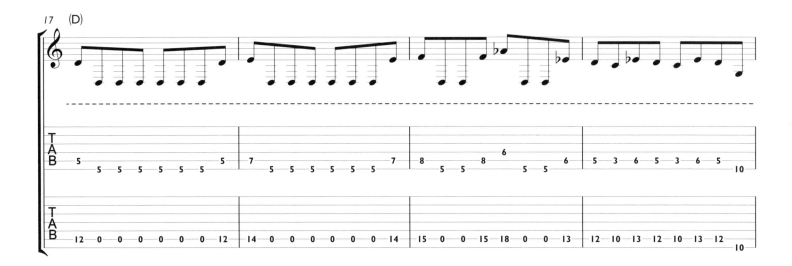

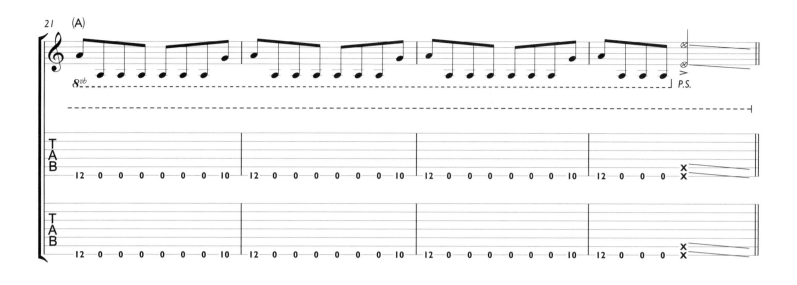

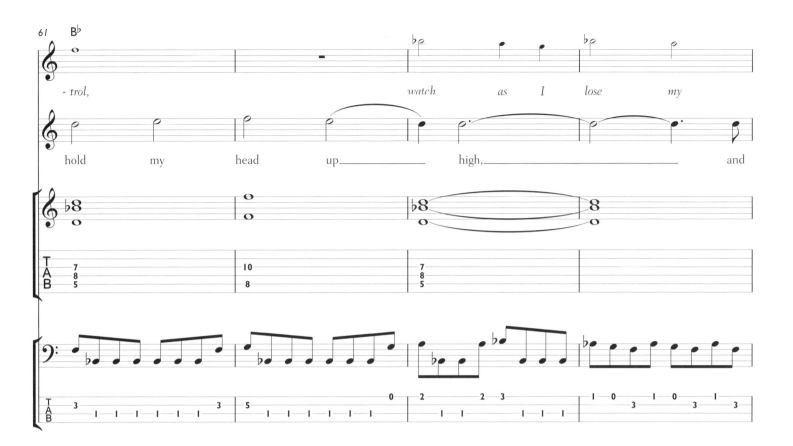

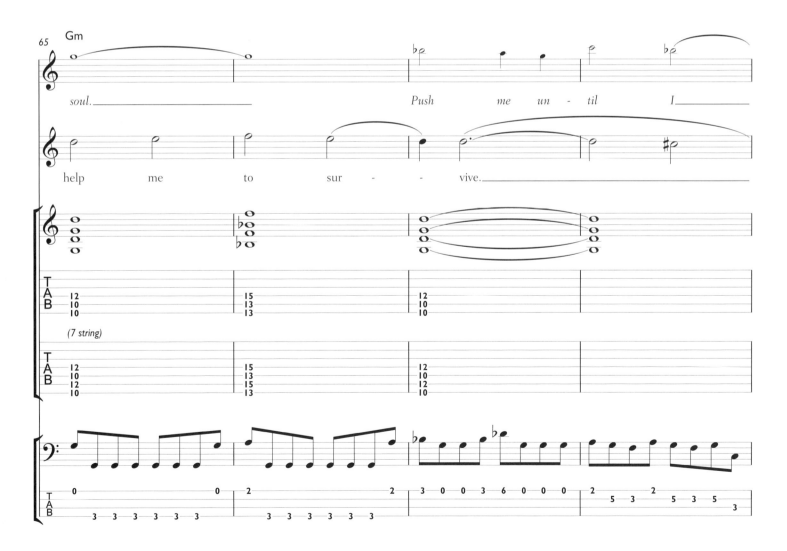

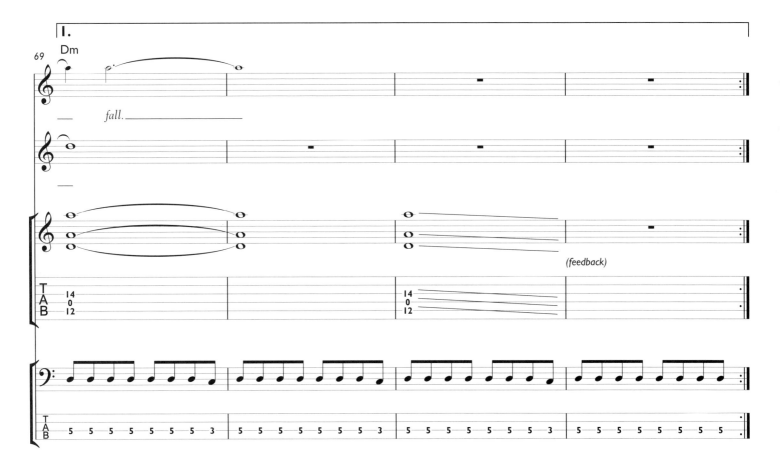

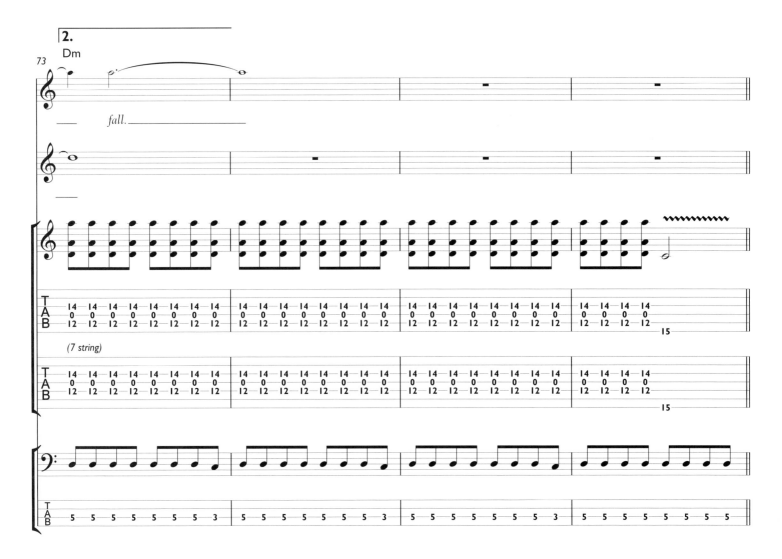

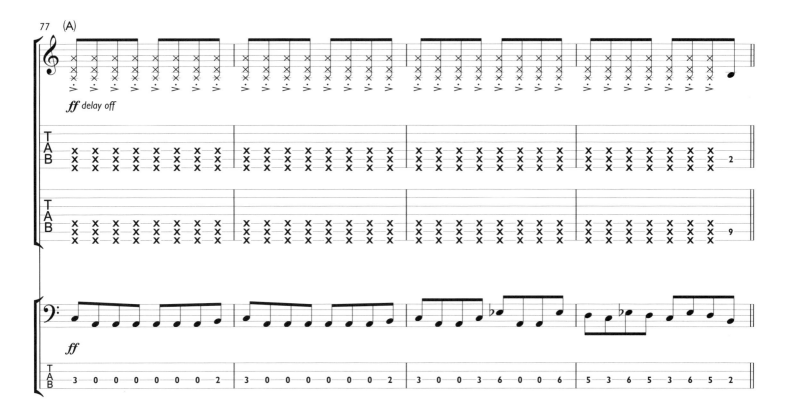

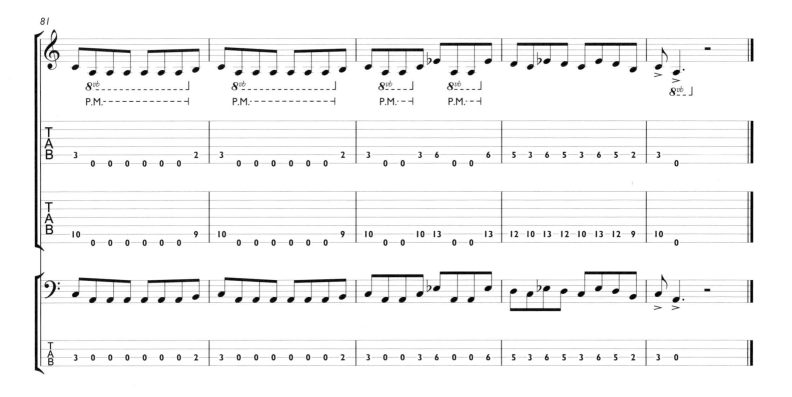

THE 2ND LAW: UNSUSTAINABLE

Words and Music by Matthew Bellamy

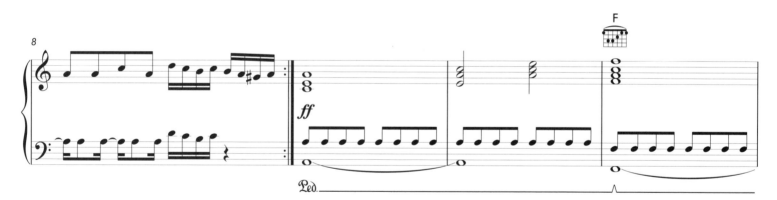

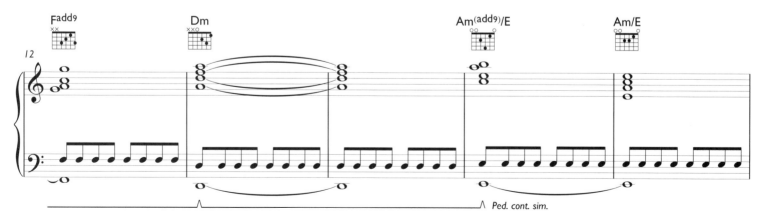

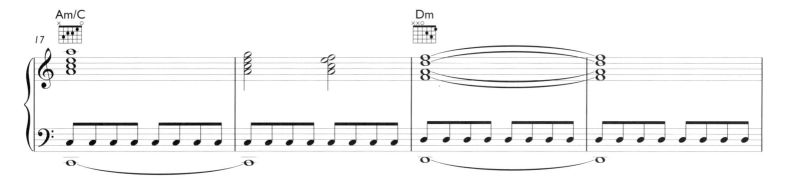

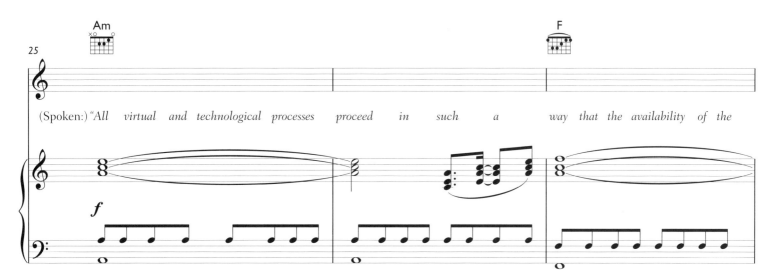

(Spoken:) "All virtual and technological processes proceed in such a way that the availability of the

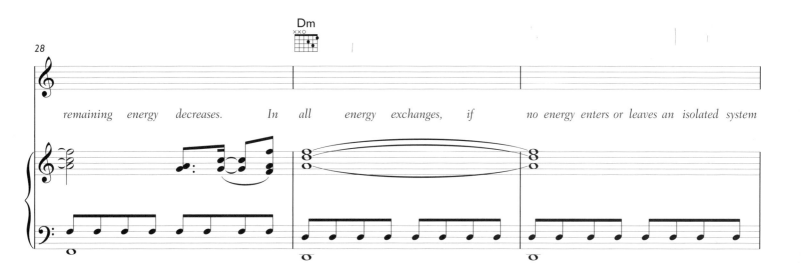

remaining energy decreases. In all energy exchanges, if no energy enters or leaves an isolated system

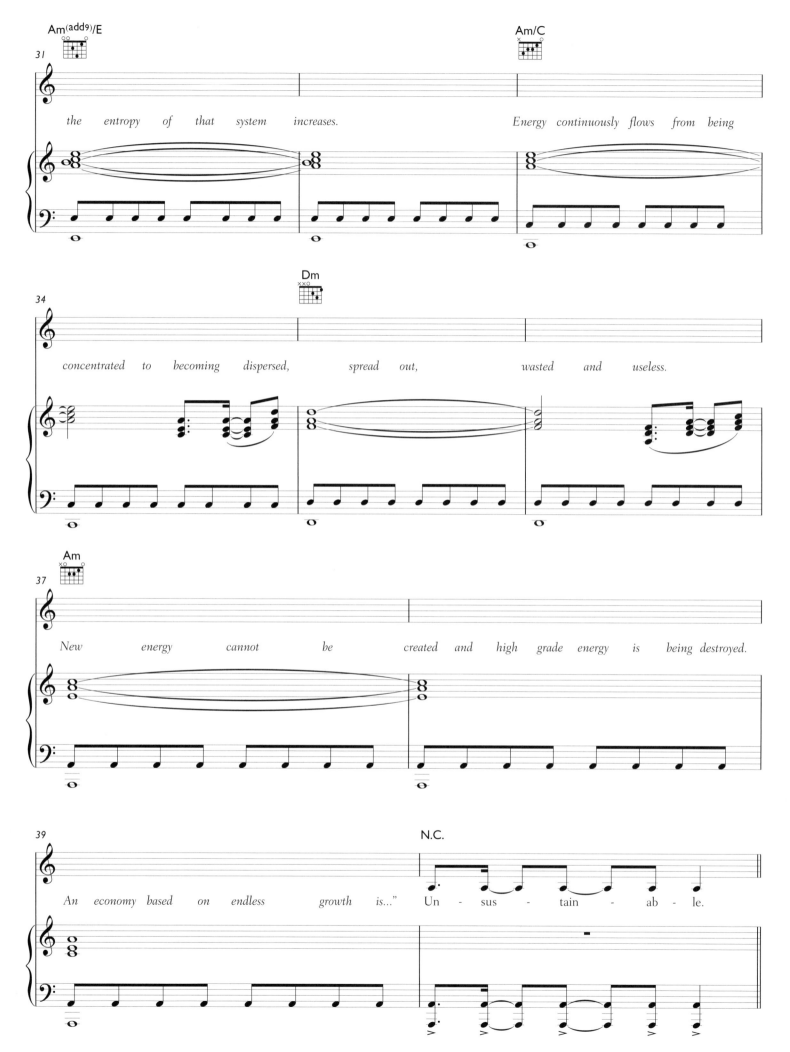

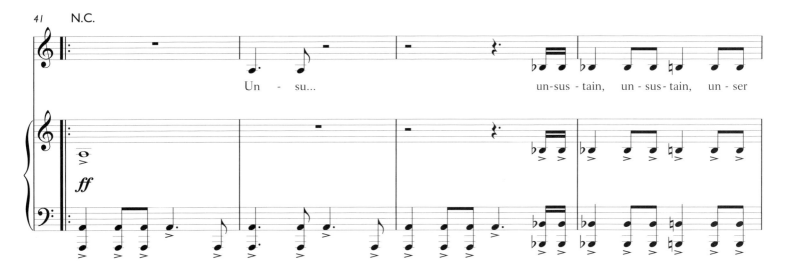

Un - su...   un-sus-tain, un-sus-tain, un-ser

un - s...   un - s...   you're un-sus-tain-ab-le, un-sus-tain-ab-le.

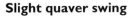

Slight quaver swing

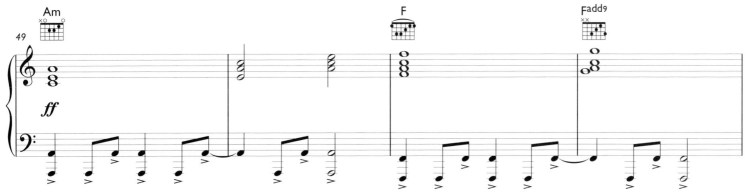

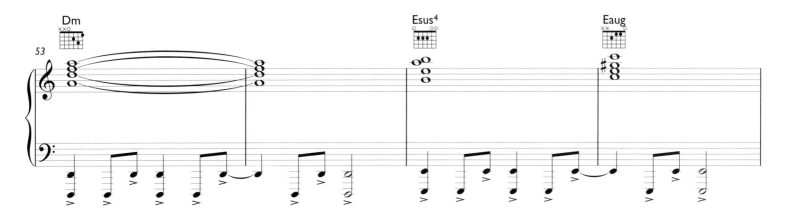

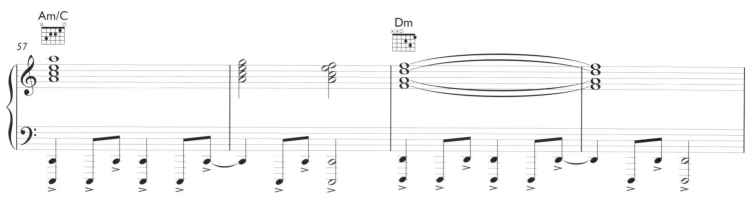

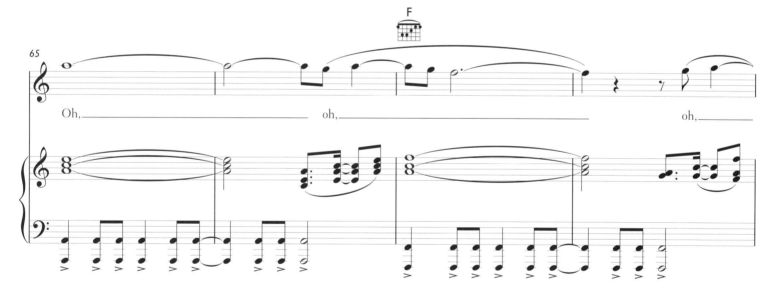

Un - sus - tain - er, un - sus - tain - er.

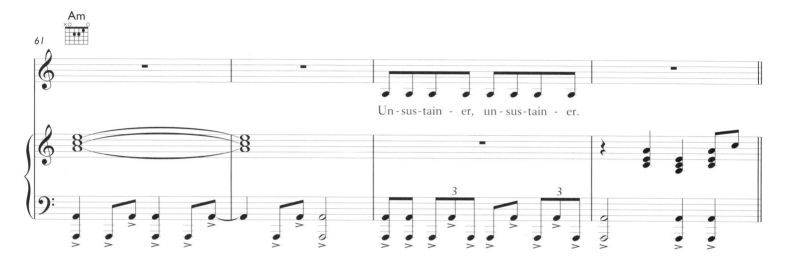

Oh,_____ oh,_____ oh,_____

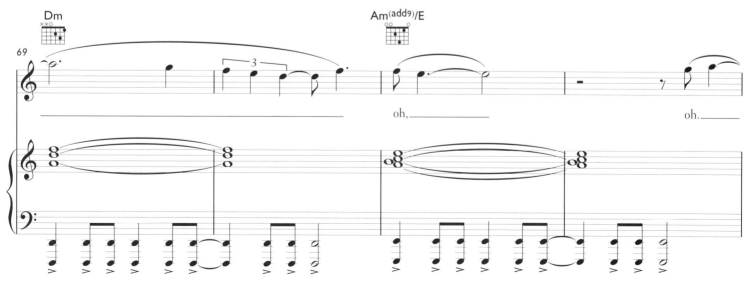

_____ oh,_____ oh._____

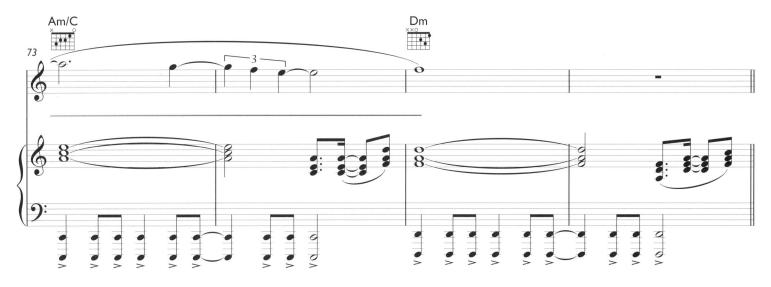

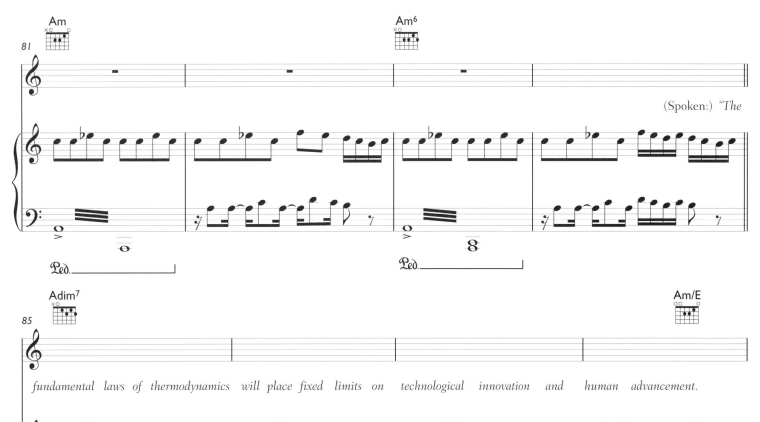

(Spoken:) "The

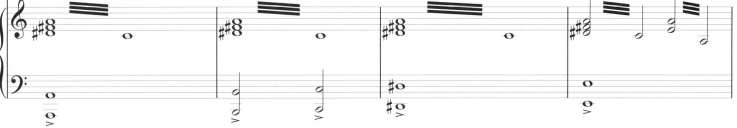

fundamental laws of thermodynamics will place fixed limits on technological innovation and human advancement.

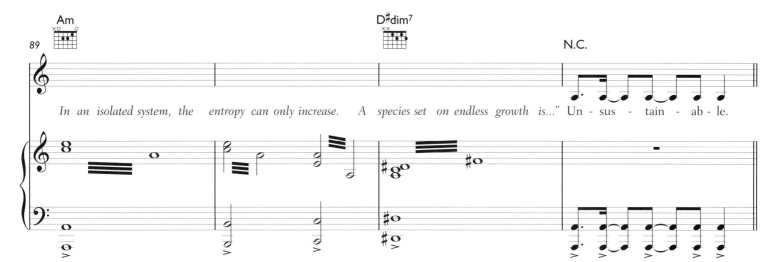

In an isolated system, the entropy can only increase. A species set on endless growth is..." Un - sus - tain - ab - le.

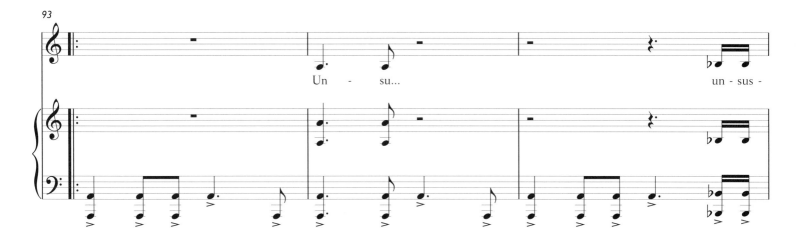

Un - su... un - sus -

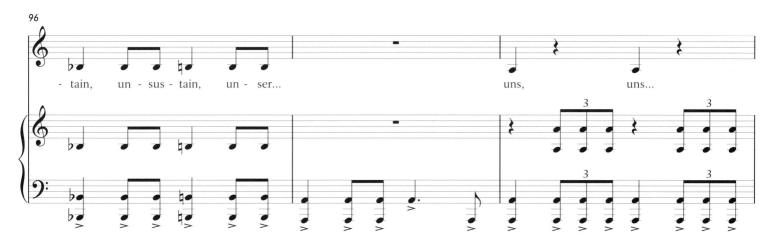

- tain, un - sus - tain, un - ser... uns, uns...

Un - sus - tain - er, un - sus - tain - er. you're un - sus - tain - ab - le.

THE 2ND LAW: ISOLATED SYSTEM

Words and Music by Matthew Bellamy

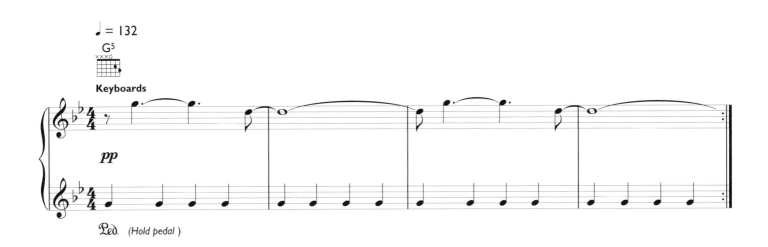

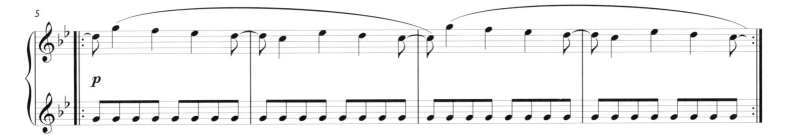

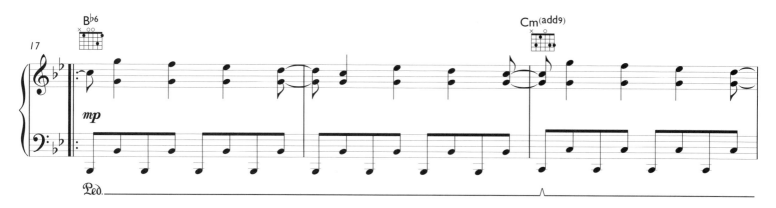

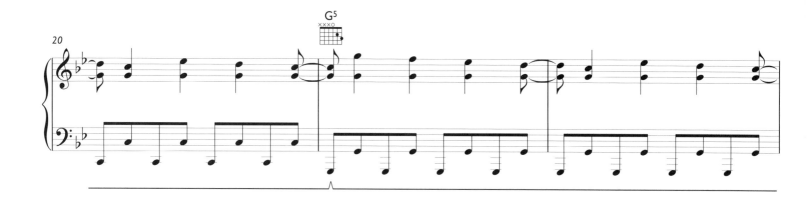

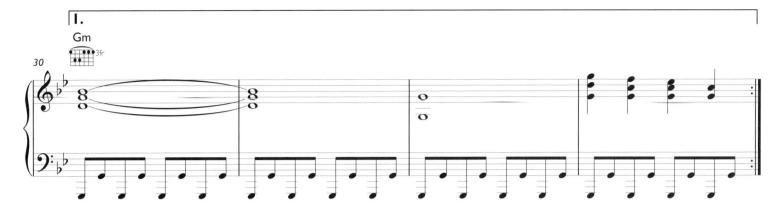

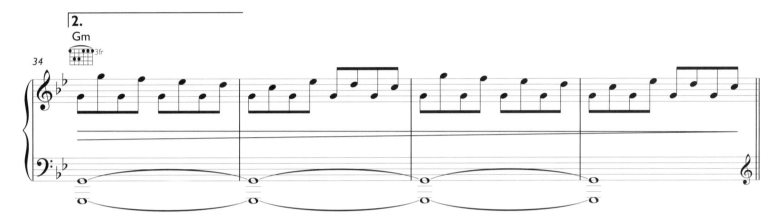

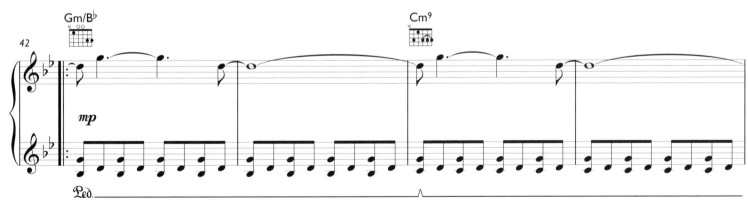

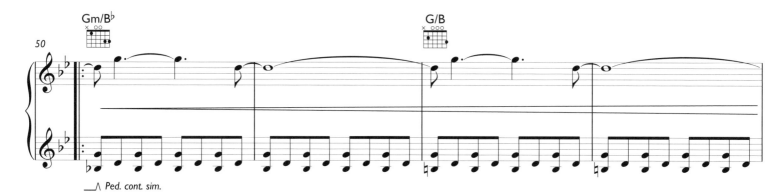

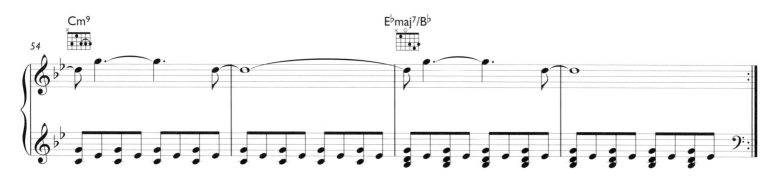

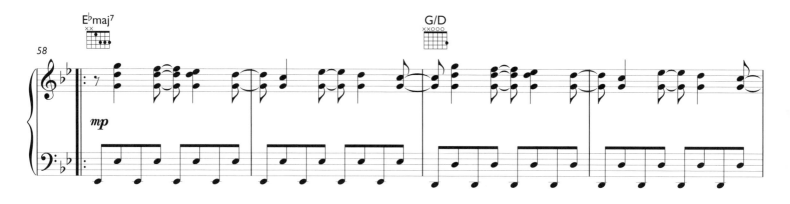

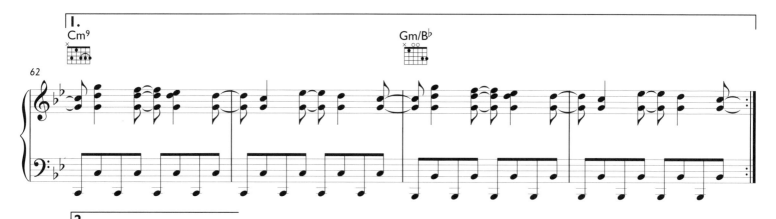

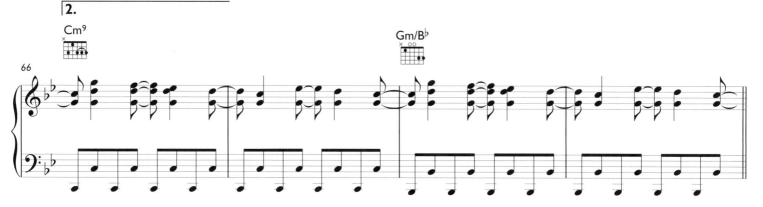

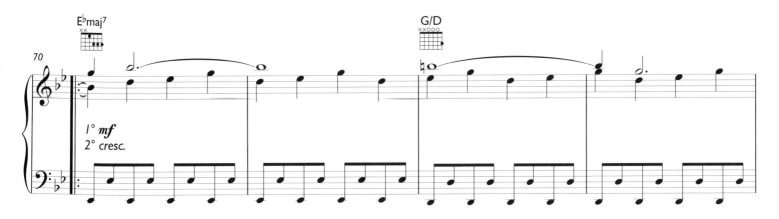

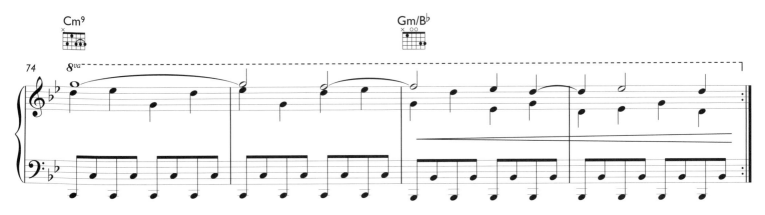

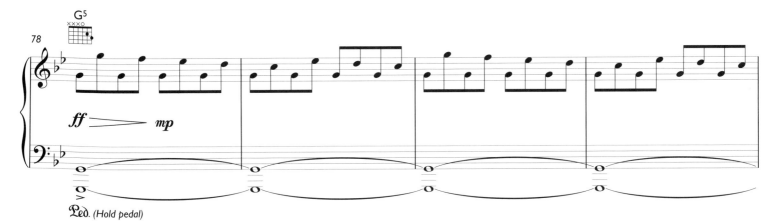

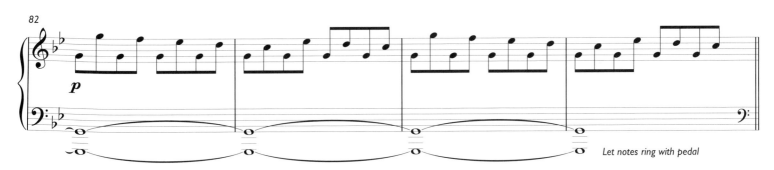

RECORDED VERSIONS®

The Best Note-For-Note Transcriptions Available

ALL BOOKS INCLUDE TABLATURE

14037551 AC/DC – Backtracks $32.99	00701764 Guitar Tab White Pages – Play-Along $39.99	00690670 Queensryche – Very Best of........................$19.95
00692015 Aerosmith – Greatest Hits......................$22.95	00694854 Buddy Guy – Damn Right, I've Got the Blues ...$19.95	00690878 The Raconteurs – Broken Boy Soldiers $19.95
00690178 Alice in Chains – Acoustic $19.95	00690840 Ben Harper – Both Sides of the Gun $19.95	00694910 Rage Against the Machine........................$19.95
00694865 Alice in Chains – Dirt $19.95	00694798 George Harrison – Anthology....................$19.95	00690055 Red Hot Chili Peppers –
00690812 All American Rejects – Move Along $19.95	00690841 Scott Henderson – Blues Guitar Collection ..$19.95	Blood Sugar Sex Magik.....................$19.95
00690958 Duane Allman Guitar Anthology $24.99	00692930 Jimi Hendrix – Are You Experienced?............$24.95	00690584 Red Hot Chili Peppers – By the Way $19.95
00694932 Allman Brothers Band – Volume 1 ....$24.95	00692931 Jimi Hendrix – Axis: Bold As Love $22.95	00691166 Red Hot Chili Peppers – I'm with You $22.99
00694933 Allman Brothers Band – Volume 2 ....$24.95	00692932 Jimi Hendrix – Electric Ladyland...............$24.95	00690852 Red Hot Chili Peppers –Stadium Arcadium ..$24.95
00694934 Allman Brothers Band – Volume 3 ....$24.95	00690017 Jimi Hendrix – Live at Woodstock $24.95	00690511 Django Reinhardt – Definitive Collection......$19.95
00690865 Atreyu – A Deathgrip on Yesterday $19.95	00690602 Jimi Hendrix – Smash Hits $24.99	00690779 Relient K – MMHMM $19.95
00690609 Audioslave...$19.95	00691152 West Coast Seattle Boy:	00690631 Rolling Stones – Guitar Anthology $27.95
00690820 Avenged Sevenfold – City of Evil $24.95	The Jimi Hendrix Anthology $29.99	00694976 Rolling Stones – Some Girls $22.95
00691065 Avenged Sevenfold – Waking the Fallen $22.99	00690793 John Lee Hooker Anthology $24.99	00690264 The Rolling Stones – Tattoo You $19.95
00690503 Beach Boys – Very Best of $19.95	00690692 Billy Idol – Very Best of........................$19.95	00690685 David Lee Roth – Eat 'Em and Smile $19.95
00690489 Beatles – 1 ....$24.99	00690688 Incubus – A Crow Left of the Murder...........$19.95	00690942 David Lee Roth and the Songs of Van Halen .$19.95
00694832 Beatles – For Acoustic Guitar $22.99	00690544 Incubus – Morningview..........................$19.95	00690031 Santana's Greatest Hits $19.95
00691014 Beatles Rock Band $34.99	00690790 Iron Maiden Anthology $24.99	00690566 Scorpions – Best of..............................$22.95
00690110 Beatles – White Album (Book 1).................$19.95	00690721 Jet – Get Born $19.95	00690604 Bob Seger – Guitar Collection $19.95
00691043 Jeff Beck – Wired $19.99	00690684 Jethro Tull – Aqualung $19.95	00690803 Kenny Wayne Shepherd Band – Best of.........$19.95
00692385 Chuck Berry $19.95	00690959 John5 – Requiem $22.95	00690968 Shinedown – The Sound of Madness $22.99
00690835 Billy Talent $19.95	00690814 John5 – Songs for Sanity $19.95	00690813 Slayer – Guitar Collection $19.95
00690901 Best of Black Sabbath $19.95	00690751 John5 – Vertigo $19.95	00690733 Slipknot – Vol. 3 (The Subliminal Verses) $22.99
00690831 blink-182 – Greatest Hits $19.95	00690845 Eric Johnson – Bloom $19.95	00120004 Steely Dan – Best of.............................$24.95
00690913 Boston $19.95	00690846 Jack Johnson and Friends – Sing-A-Longs and	00694921 Steppenwolf – Best of...........................$22.95
00690932 Boston – Don't Look Back $19.99	Lullabies for the Film Curious George........$19.95	00690655 Mike Stern – Best of.............................$19.95
00690491 David Bowie – Best of $19.95	00690271 Robert Johnson – New Transcriptions $24.95	00690877 Stone Sour – Come What(ever) May $19.95
00690873 Breaking Benjamin – Phobia $19.95	00691131 Janis Joplin – Best of $19.95	00690520 Styx Guitar Collection $19.95
00690451 Jeff Buckley – Collection $24.95	00690427 Judas Priest – Best of $22.99	00120081 Sublime...$19.95
00690957 Bullet for My Valentine – Scream Aim Fire ...$22.99	00690975 Kings of Leon – Only by the Night $22.99	00120122 Sublime – 40oz. to Freedom $19.95
00691159 The Cars – Complete Greatest Hits $22.95	00694903 Kiss – Best of.................................$24.95	00690929 Sum 41 – Underclass Hero $19.95
00691079 Best of Johnny Cash $22.99	00690355 Kiss – Destroyer $16.95	00690767 Switchfoot – The Beautiful Letdown............$19.95
00691004 Chickenfoot $22.99	00690834 Lamb of God – Ashes of the Wake $19.95	00690993 Taylor Swift – Fearless..........................$22.99
00690590 Eric Clapton – Anthology........................$29.95	00690875 Lamb of God – Sacrament $19.95	00690830 System of a Down – Hypnotize $19.95
00690415 Clapton Chronicles – Best of Eric Clapton $18.95	00690823 Ray LaMontagne – Trouble $19.95	00690531 System of a Down – Toxicity $19.95
00690936 Eric Clapton – Complete Clapton $29.99	00690679 John Lennon – Guitar Collection $19.95	00694824 James Taylor – Best of...........................$16.95
00690074 Eric Clapton – The Cream of Clapton...........$24.95	00690781 Linkin Park – Hybrid Theory....................$22.95	00690871 Three Days Grace – One-X $19.95
00694869 Eric Clapton – Unplugged.......................$22.95	00690743 Los Lonely Boys $19.95	00690683 Robin Trower – Bridge of Sighs.................$19.95
00690162 The Clash – Best of.............................$19.95	00690720 Lostprophets – Start Something.................$19.95	00699191 U2 – Best of: 1980-1990 ....$19.95
00690828 Coheed & Cambria – Good Apollo I'm	00690955 Lynyrd Skynyrd – All-Time Greatest Hits $19.99	00690732 U2 – Best of: 1990-2000 ....$19.95
Burning Star, IV, Vol. 1: From Fear	00694954 Lynyrd Skynyrd – New Best of $19.95	00660137 Steve Vai – Passion & Warfare $24.95
Through the Eyes of Madness $19.95	00690754 Marilyn Manson – Lest We Forget................$19.95	00690116 Stevie Ray Vaughan – Guitar Collection.........$24.95
00690593 Coldplay – A Rush of Blood to the Head.......$19.95	00694956 Bob Marley– Legend $19.95	00660058 Stevie Ray Vaughan –
00690962 Coldplay – Viva La Vida $19.95	00694945 Bob Marley– Songs of Freedom...............$24.95	Lightnin' Blues 1983-1987 ....$24.95
00690819 Creedence Clearwater Revival – Best of.........$22.95	00690657 Maroon5 – Songs about Jane $19.95	00694835 Stevie Ray Vaughan – The Sky Is Crying $22.95
00690648 The Very Best of Jim Croce $19.95	00120080 Don McLean – Songbook $19.95	00690015 Stevie Ray Vaughan – Texas Flood $19.95
00690613 Crosby, Stills & Nash – Best of..................$22.95	00694951 Megadeth – Rust in Peace $22.95	00690772 Velvet Revolver – Contraband...................$22.95
00690967 Death Cab for Cutie – Narrow Stairs $22.99	00691185 Megadeth – Th1rt3en $22.99	00690071 Weezer (The Blue Album) $19.95
00690289 Deep Purple – Best of $19.99	00690951 Megadeth – United Abominations $22.99	00690966 Weezer – (Red Album) $19.99
00690784 Def Leppard – Best of $19.95	00690505 John Mellencamp – Guitar Collection...........$19.95	00690447 The Who – Best of..............................$24.95
00692240 Bo Diddley $19.99	00690646 Pat Metheny – One Quiet Night..................$19.95	00690916 The Best of Dwight Yoakam $19.95
00690347 The Doors – Anthology..........................$22.95	00690558 Pat Metheny – Trio: 99>00 ....$19.95	00690905 Neil Young – Rust Never Sleeps $19.99
00690348 The Doors – Essential Guitar Collection $16.95	00690040 Steve Miller Band – Young Hearts $19.95	00690623 Frank Zappa – Over-Nite Sensation $22.99
00691186 Evanescence $19.95	00691070 Mumford & Sons – Sigh No More $22.99	00690589 ZZ Top Guitar Anthology.........................$24.95
00690810 Fall Out Boy – From Under the Cork Tree.....$19.95	00694883 Nirvana – Nevermind $19.95	
00691181 Five Finger Death Punch –	00690026 Nirvana – Unplugged in New York $19.95	
American Capitalist $22.99	00690807 The Offspring – Greatest Hits $19.95	
00690664 Fleetwood Mac – Best of $19.95	00694847 Ozzy Osbourne – Best of $22.95	
00690870 Flyleaf $19.95	00690399 Ozzy Osbourne – Ozzman Cometh...............$22.99	
00690931 Foo Fighters – Echoes, Silence,	00690933 Best of Brad Paisley $22.95	
Patience & Grace $19.95	00690995 Brad Paisley – Play: The Guitar Album $24.99	
00690808 Foo Fighters – In Your Honor $19.95	00694855 Pearl Jam – Ten.................................$22.99	
00691115 Foo Fighters – Wasting Light $22.99	00690439 A Perfect Circle – Mer De Noms $19.95	
00690805 Robben Ford – Best of $22.95	00690499 Tom Petty – Definitive Guitar Collection.......$19.95	
00694920 Free – Best of....................................$19.95	00690428 Pink Floyd – Dark Side of the Moon $19.95	
00691050 Glee Guitar Collection $19.99	00690789 Poison – Best of.................................$19.95	
00690943 The Goo Goo Dolls – Greatest Hits	00693864 The Police – Best of..............................$19.95	
Volume 1: The Singles $22.95	00694975 Queen – Greatest Hits..........................$24.95	

Prices and availability subject to change without notice.
Some products may not be available outside the U.S.A.

0812